Foreword by Nancy Alcorn
Founder and President of Mercy Ministries

MOTHER Are You Sitting Down?

God's Astounding Answers to a Family's Crisis

LISA BAKER ■ JAIME BAKER LOWERY

MOTHER
Are You Sitting Down?

MOTHER
Are You Sitting Down?

God's Astounding Answers to a Family's Crisis

LISA BAKER ■ JAIME BAKER LOWERY

Copyright © 2013 by Lisa Baker and Jaime Baker Lowery

All rights reserved. No part of this book may be used or reproduced in any manner, stored in a retrieval system, or transmitted in any form or by any means – electronic, mechanical, photocopy, recording, scanning or any other – except in the case of brief quotations in printed reviews, without the prior written permission from the Authors.

Unless otherwise indicated, all Scripture quotations are taken from the *Holy Bible, New International Version* ®, copyright © 1973, 1987, 1984 by International Bible Society. Used by permission of Zondervan. All rights reserved.

Scripture quotations marked AMP are taken from *The Amplified Bible, Old Testament*, copyright © 1965, 1987 by the Zondervan Corporation. *The Amplified New Testament*, copyright 1958, 1987, by the Lockman Foundation. Used by permission.

Scripture quotations marked NKJ are taken from *The New King James Version of the Bible*, Copyright © 1979, 1980 by Tomas Nelson, Inc., Publishers. Used by permission.

Drawbaugh Publishing Group
444 Allen Drive
Chambersburg, PA 17202

Paperback ISBN 978-0-9892680-3-5
eBook ISBN 978-0-9892680-4-2

For Worldwide Distribution, Printed in the United States.

1 2 3 4 5 6 7 8 9 10 / 17 16 15 14 13

Endorsements

❧ ☙

A riveting story of two women who valiantly walked through some of life's most challenging events. Each one experienced the impact of human frailty, while discovering the empowering strength of God's extravagant love. As the reader journeys through the story, Christ's redemptive blood can be seen kissing every page with the assurance that *all things work together for good to those who love God, to those who are called according to His purpose.*

An incredible must read book for all who value the preciousness of life and for those who need to know there is *no such thing as a no way out situation.*

> *Trust in the* LORD *with all your heart,*
> *And lean not on your own understanding;*
> *In all your ways acknowledge Him,*
> *And He shall direct your paths. Proverbs 3:5-6*

Lisa and Jaime not only believed, but also courageously walked this scripture out paving the way for many to follow in the footsteps, which lead to life!

Dave and Dee Dee Thompson
Senior Pastors, Activation Ministry Center

Mother, Are You Sitting Down? Simply reading the title draws me to this heartwarming, honest, and beautifully written book. Lisa and Jaime, mother and daughter, write together about their journey, approaching

Endorsements

the topics of unplanned pregnancy and adoption with great insight and hope. This is a wonderful book, celebrating LIFE!

Rebecca St. James
Grammy and Dove award recipient
Best-selling author

"Mother Are You Sitting Down?" is a poignant story of redemption. Lisa Baker and her daughter Jaime Baker Lowery tell of their relationship as mother and daughter during a heart-wrenching season as Jaime transitioned from adolescence into adulthood. Their journey with God is woven into the fabric of their lives as this story of love and healing unfolds.

Rev. Laura Beach
Founder & Director of Equipping Lydia Ministry

Deeply moving. Heart wrenching. Faith renewing. In this family's story of their journey through the heights and depths of every emotion, you'll see the hand and grace of God. You'll see God's love expressed in such tender ways through a mother's love—Jaime's love for her son and Lisa's love for Jaime. This book is amazing and I believe God will touch many hearts and change many lives through it. What comes pouring out during the crises and trials of our lives show what's really inside, and it's obvious each one has a genuine, deep walk with God. The Father's love and the Spirit of Jesus pour out of every page!

Rev. Tommy Hays
Founder of Messiah Ministries

You will be captivated by the faith in God's Word the Baker family displays throughout every page of this story. As a mother, sister in the Lord and friend of these precious women, it was an honor to walk, learn, pray and heal with them during the writing of this book. You cannot read this without feeling their sorrow, pain and complete dependence upon our Lord and King, Jesus Christ. The Holy Spirit guided every word and as a result you, too, will be offered the Joy of healing associated with believing that God's Word is perfect for everyday life. The fruits of this book are many; I fully expect it to touch lives around the world. It is a MUST to read; you won't want to put it down!

Brenda B. Everman
Lay Pastor, United Methodist Church

Acknowledgments

༄ ༅

First and foremost, our most profound gratitude to our Lord and Savior, without whom there would be no story. Your unconditional love, grace and mercy overwhelmed us as we witnessed it come to life. We continue to be in complete awe of you as the story and its lessons speak to us repeatedly and bless so many others. We delight in being your daughters and love you dearly!

Our deepest appreciation to our family and friends and to those who labored with us in prayer, undergirding us during this project. We couldn't have done this without your constant love and support along the way.

To Dan and Kari, your friendship and support has been precious to us. We're immensely grateful for the openness with your family over the years and the closeness we share today.

Lisa and Jaime

To Jeremy, thank you for being there for me over the years, offering your deepest love, genuine support and infinite encouragement. I can always count on you, with your sound advice and godly wisdom, to speak the truth. I am truly honored to be your wife and am exceptionally grateful I have the privilege of spending the rest of my days by your side. I love you dearly, my husband and truest friend.

Jaime

Acknowledgments

To my husband and sweetheart, Gene, this book would not be a reality, had it not been for your gentle nudging and encouragement during the years it took to write. I am deeply grateful for your unwavering love and friendship. You are precious to me and I love you with all my heart!

Lisa

Table of Contents

༄ ༅

Acknowledgments 7

Foreword 11

CHAPTER 1 - *Mother's Day* 13

CHAPTER 2 - *The News* 19

CHAPTER 3 - *A Rough Start* 23

CHAPTER 4 - *Mercy* 27

CHAPTER 5 - *An Emotional Ride* 33

CHAPTER 6 - *Letting Go* 37

CHAPTER 7 - *Turning Point* 41

CHAPTER 8 - *A Divine Appointment* 45

CHAPTER 9 - *Mercy Ministries* 53

CHAPTER 10 - *Embracing Change* 61

CHAPTER 11 - *God Kisses* 65

CHAPTER 12 - *Dreaming with God* 73

Table of Contents

CHAPTER 13 – *Back to Nashville*.. 79
CHAPTER 14 – *Caught Off Guard*.. 85
CHAPTER 15 – *The Waiting Game*... 95
CHAPTER 16 – *It Begins* 101
CHAPTER 17 – *Brennan's Birth* 109
CHAPTER 18 – *Gift of God* 113
CHAPTER 19 – *The Scare* 119
CHAPTER 20 – *Cherished Moments*... 125
CHAPTER 21 – *Surrender Day* 129
CHAPTER 22 – *Life Afterwards*.. 137
CHAPTER 23 – *Family Christmas*... 145
CHAPTER 24 – *Adoption Ceremony*... 149
CHAPTER 25 – *Wrapping Up* 153
CHAPTER 26 – *Full Circle*.. 155

Author's Notes.. 159

Foreword

For more than 30 years I have had the privilege of working with thousands of young women who have walked through the doors of Mercy Ministries—desperate, hurting, and feeling alone. I have always been especially close to the young women who enter our program with an unplanned pregnancy, because when I first started Mercy, I received a direct word from God that I was to tell every pregnant young woman how proud He was of them for choosing life.

My heart is so moved when young women have the courage and strength to not only choose life, but to actually come to a place where they can receive training and be given all of the options for parenting or placing their baby for adoption. God showed me that our job is to lead each woman—young or older—into a personal relationship with Christ and allow Him to lead her in the decision of whether to place for adoption or parent.

Looking back, I will forever remember August 8, 2002. A young woman named Jaime walked through our doors not knowing anyone, yet knowing that God had brought her to this place to make one of the most difficult decisions she would ever have to face. I remember being struck by the fact that Jaime had such a close-knit family, and witnessing firsthand how difficult it was for her mom, Lisa, to leave her at Mercy Ministries. It never ceases to amaze me when such wonderful families allow their faith in God to entrust their daughters to the care of Mercy. I did not know Jaime's full story on that August day in 2002, but I would soon find out that Jaime had come very close to aborting her child, which is one of the most compelling parts of the heart-touching story you are about to read.

Many of the families we work with at Mercy are extremely broken, but Jaime comes from a strong Christian family, where everyone is very close to one another and fully supportive of each other. However, no matter how things may appear, no family is completely perfect or exempt from struggle. What happened in Jaime's life and the life of her family during her stay at Mercy is nothing short of a miracle, which is what makes this story so beautiful and redemptive. It is definitely a story that I believe every family should read.

Nancy Alcorn
Founder and President of Mercy Ministries
Nashville, Tennessee

Chapter 1

Mother's Day

Lisa

 The hot Arizona sun scorched the already parched air, creating the perfect dry sauna. It was 112 degrees. There was no relief in sight and not a single cloud graced the pale blue sky. My family and I labored in those conditions, finishing a yard renovation project as a Mother's Day gift for our elderly mother.

 My husband, Gene, and I arrived earlier in the week having left our home in the refreshingly cool Colorado Rockies to make the two-day drive to Scottsdale. We started the prep work early Friday morning before being joined by a sister and brother and their families later that afternoon. The plan was to complete as much as we could by the end of the weekend. I would wrap up any remaining work, visit for a few extra days, and then fly back home midweek.

 It had already been a long, exhausting weekend, and it wasn't over yet. Worn out, everyone had gone home after dinner Saturday except for Gene and me, who were staying there at Mother's.

 Early Sunday morning, we joined Mother for breakfast and Gene wished us both a Happy Mother's Day. He needed to leave right away to be home that night, both for work and to celebrate our daughter's 20th birthday with her the next day. This was the first year I wouldn't be with Jaime on her actual birthday, and I hated that. However, it was the only weekend the family could gather to do this project for Mother before the hottest summer months arrived, and she needed the help and the joy we hoped it would bring her. Jaime assured me it was okay and that we could celebrate all together when I returned.

As soon as Gene left, I started back to work on the yard, taking advantage of the cooler temperatures of the early morning. Mother had not been feeling well lately and I hoped that when she gazed out she would enjoy the beautiful flowers and greenery we planted; that they would brighten her day and lift her spirits.

I had been working for some time when she came outside to visit with me for a few minutes and brought the phone with her. She needed to run to the grocery store and thought I would like to have it close by in case it rang so I wouldn't have to stop and wipe off dirt and mud before I ran inside to answer it. I smiled, thinking about how much I loved her.

Soon after she left, the phone rang, jolting me from my thoughts. Grateful for the interruption, I wiped my forehead, rubbed my dirty hands on my shorts, grabbed my water bottle, and headed over to the corner of the yard, sitting down under a large tree. Thank goodness for the shade.

The call was from Jaime, who was taking time off from college and had moved back to town. She was house-sitting for Gene and me while we were gone and had called Wednesday, shortly after we left. From the tone in her voice that day, I sensed something wasn't quite right, but when I questioned her about it, she claimed she was fine and that she would take good care of everything and not to worry. So we prayed for her and continued on our trip, concerned, but aware there wasn't anything else we could do right then. I did what I had learned to do over the years; turn her over to the Lord and entrust her and whatever was going on into His hands.

I called her Friday morning and heard it again. There was definitely something wrong, but once more, she dismissed my concern saying she wasn't feeling well. She was taking the day off from work, but it was nothing to worry about. So I lifted up another prayer for her.

After a little small-talk, Jaime wished me a Happy Mother's Day and told me how she wished we could be together for it. Then she asked me the question that pierced my heart:

"Mother, are you sitting down?"

I wish I could describe the thoughts and feelings that flew through my mind and heart in that next millisecond. *Oh, no!* In that deep place inside my heart, I already knew what she was about to say.

"Yes, I'm sitting down."

Then in a faltering voice, interjected with sobs and tears, she said,

"Mother...I'm...pregnant."

I went completely numb. A horrible feeling began gnawing at the pit of my stomach. Time, the world, everything around me stopped utterly still and lost its color. I felt paralyzed.

I couldn't get my mind to think, much less my lips to form words, however, I knew I needed to say *something*. I needed to respond and I realized my reply, my attitude and the heart behind it, combined into the next several words I spoke, were critically important. They could either make or break her, the situation we now faced, our future relationship as mother and daughter, and even her own relationship to her Heavenly Father. They would either strengthen and lift her, empowering her to walk through what was to come, or crush her further, sending her even deeper into despair. I could not answer with the anger and hurt and pain I was suddenly experiencing, or the accusations or judgment that might have come rushing out of my mouth. No, she needed to hear what her heart desperately required: my unconditional love.

Lord, help! What do I say? Immediately, my dear friend, Connie, came to mind, along with the exact words she spoke when she heard the same thing from her teenage daughter several years before. I had admired the wisdom of her gentle and loving response. Grateful for this reminder, I consciously turned from my numb thoughts and with as much love and tenderness as I could muster, I replied just as she had:

"Oh, Honey...I'm so sorry.
I love you so much....
I wish I were there to just hold you and hug you..."

I let her cry and then asked her to tell me about what had happened. I wanted her to tell me how she knew, when she found out, and any other details she wanted me to know about, all the time trying to keep the door wide open for her to share her hurt with me and sense my deep love. She found out shortly after Gene and I left town and had known all this time, dealing with the pain of it by herself; waiting for a good time to tell us.

Before we finished the call I told her again how much I loved her, how sorry I was and that I wished I could be there with her.

After we hung up, finding myself suddenly back in the real world gave me the strangest feeling. In an instant, everything in my own personal world had changed dramatically, but nothing here in this one had at all. I was still at Mother's, miles from home, with an incredible amount of yard work to still do. I also desperately needed to have someone to share the burden of Jaime's news with, but Jaime asked me to keep it to myself, so I was completely alone with all my feelings.

Hot, drained and numb; almost sick to my stomach and reeling with this news, all I wanted to do was to go upstairs into the room, close the door and…I didn't know what. I just knew I had to be alone with it and with the Lord. I sank to my knees and bowed over them with my face in my hands and sobbed a deep, long, wracking cry. The pain and the grief were simply too much for words.

I don't know how long I was there, but after a while the first wave subsided and I realized that I had, without a word, poured it all out to the Lord. When I could, I got up, splashed some water on my face and went back outside to press on with the work.

I went about my tasks in the garden on autopilot. It wasn't until mid-afternoon that I realized no one had returned to help. I pondered what had happened and it finally occurred to me everyone must be celebrating Mother's Day with their families. We hadn't actually discussed working that day. I'd just assumed we would, since we had a good part of the day available and there was still so much left to do.

Disheartened and overwhelmed, I took note of the remaining work and realized that even with help, I would have to work really hard until the end of the week to wrap it all up.

Soggy with rivulets of perspiration trickling down my face and weak from the prospect of what lay before me, I finally decided I had better make a major attitude adjustment. I would add a few days to my trip, and make it more enjoyable by spending extra time visiting with Mother, family, and a few good friends while in town.

A little while later I was able to reach Gene on his cell phone as he was driving back to Colorado. I desperately needed to talk to him, but knowing Jaime needed to tell him the news herself—and she wanted to do it in person—I held back and only made small talk. She had asked me to let him know she needed to talk to him about something important when he got home that night. I knew it would be a difficult conversation for both of them. Jaime has always been Daddy's little girl, and they have enjoyed a very special relationship. When he asked me what she wanted to talk about, I simply said she would fill him in on everything when he arrived and that we could talk later.

That evening, Mother and I met my sister, Liz, and her family for dinner. It was difficult joining into the conversations or the joy of the occasion with the deep secret I carried. I felt as if I were trapped in another world adjacent to this one—like that old TV show "The Twilight Zone.

I've never missed any of Jaime's birthdays or Mother's Days! Why in the world did it have to be this one, this year?! I need to be home with her—and with Gene!

… Chapter 2

The News

❦ ❧

Jaime

Friday before Mother's Day, I woke up at 6:30 a.m. to get ready for work. I had been feeling ill for days but didn't think too much of it until a couple of coworkers mentioned they had noticed it the last several mornings and wondered if it could be morning sickness. At first I shrugged off the idea, but I had never quite felt like this before, so reluctantly, I bought a home pregnancy test just to make sure.

I didn't want to take it. *Did I really have to know?* Surely this was so silly; me thinking I was pregnant. *But still, what if I were? What in the world would I do?* I started getting nervous and scared, but I forced myself to take it. I had no idea my life was about to change…forever.

As I looked at the results, I thought I was seeing them wrong. *No…No…* I kept looking back and forth from them to the instructions. *This can't be right! The instructions are misprinted or something!* Tears welled up in my eyes and I let out a huge cry. *Noooo!!* Devastated, I sobbed hysterically for several minutes. This couldn't be happening to me.

It felt like a dream I kept expecting to wake up from. At some point, though, the reality of it all started to set in. My thoughts progressed from one to the next. Questions, so many questions, and I had no answers. *Oh my gosh, what are my parents going to say? What am I going to do?! I am so young and have my whole life in front of me. I'm not ready to be a mother!! Am I going to parent this child alone? Should I just have an abortion? I can't believe I'm thinking that! But how am I going to provide for this child? How am I going to continue working when I have a child? Does this mean I will never get married? What if no one wants to marry me since I have a child?! My life is ruined!*

I must have looked like a crazy woman. From room to room I went, frantically sobbing; crying out to God. *Why me! Why, Lord. Why?* Finally, I went into my parents' room and fell face down on their bed and wept for I don't know how long.

I rarely missed a day of work, but that day there was no way I could go. I was a complete mess. When my manager answered the phone, I tried my best to pull it together and sound as professional as I could. "I'm not going to be able to make it in today." She could hear my voice cracking and sweetly asked if I were okay. I couldn't hold it back and began crying again as I told her I just found out I was pregnant. She obviously knew this was a shock to me and said she was so sorry. She told me to take the weekend and rest, and to let her know if there was anything she could do for me and she would see me on Monday.

Over the next couple of hours I didn't call anyone. I curled up in my parents' bed and cried myself to sleep, hoping I would wake up to find out this was all a terrible dream.

Then the phone rang. It was Mom. *Oh, how I so wish you were here!* There was no way I could tell her the news right now, and especially not on the phone. She had a quick question and was going to leave a voicemail thinking I would be at work, but to her surprise I answered her call. She could tell instantly something was amiss and asked why I was able to answer. I reassured her I was fine but that I wasn't feeling well so I took the day off work. There was nothing to worry about.

Later that morning I decided I needed to have a blood test in case the home pregnancy test was wrong. I called my good friend, Jen, to see if she would be willing to go with me. I knew she would be off work that day and I desperately needed a friend with me. She, as well as my other close friends, were supportive and loving when I told them the news. They were a godsend, especially during those few days before Dad came home.

The rest of the day and all day Saturday were a blur. Between the numbness I felt and the weeping, I was in survival mode, just trying to get through.

Telling my parents would be the hardest thing I would ever have to say to them. I knew it would be sobering and humiliating. Like me, they would be heartbroken by the news and probably upset, embarrassed, and ashamed. I was afraid this would taint the community's view of our family and ruin our Christian reputation. The last thing I wanted to do was to bring dishonor to our family.

I didn't want to tell Mom over the phone, and especially not on Mother's Day. But I would be talking with Dad when he got home the next night and, although I dreaded it, I desperately needed to tell them both.

I called her midday and told her how much I loved her; that I was thinking about her and missing her. When I broke the news, Mom was obviously in shock and terribly disappointed, but she still responded with deep love and concern for me—exactly the response I needed in that moment.

Not long after Dad arrived home, I asked if I could talk to him and we sat down at the dining room table. I had carried this burden for two days by myself. Although I knew it would also be on his shoulders the moment I told him and that he would be justifiably upset, he would show how much he loved me, and that love was what I needed so badly. I yearned for my father to wrap me up in his arms and tell me everything was going to be okay; that we would get through this somehow.

That moment is still so vivid. As we sat at the dining room table he asked what was on my mind. At first I didn't know how to break the news to him. So after a few moments of trying to figure out what to say, I muttered,

"Dad, probably the worst thing that you ever thought would happen to me has happened."

I hoped he would catch on but he waited for me to say it. He later told me he knew exactly what I was going to tell him, but he wanted it to come from me.

He calmly responded, "What do you mean?" Then he waited for my response.

With a deep breath, I somehow formed the words,

"Dad, I'm pregnant."

He paused a brief moment to take the words in, but then looked at me with great compassion and love in his eyes. He reached out, brought me close, and held me as I cried in his arms. He told me how much he loved me; that he wished this had not happened but that he forgave me and we would get through this.

My journal entry for that day read:

"My parents had to endure the worst news of their lives today. To my astonishment, they didn't disown me; they actually showed me more love and grace than I thought was humanly possible."

✌ ✍

Lisa

Gene is really good at waiting. It's one of his strengths. He told me the thoughts that came to him during the silence that followed Jaime's announcement: *What do I do here? There are two ways to go; to forgive her and love her, or to get mad, and show my anger and deep disappointment.*

Now, Gene is not a man to get angry. He is the calm, steady type; solid and deeply grounded. I think I've seen him angry perhaps two times in our marriage. For him to react that way would have been out of character. However, that didn't mean he never got angry; he has just learned how to handle it. Even though he told me he had a sense about what she was going to say and was able to pray and prepare himself a little before he arrived at home, it still shocked him. Afraid he might not say the right words, he remembered trying to look into the future to see what it all might look like. The most important thing right then was for him to tell her he loved her and that we'd get through it. He also wondered what she had been going through these last few days, having to handle it alone; and he hurt for her.

It helped tremendously to talk to Gene, to share the heavy load and hear the same thoughts had come to his mind and that we had chosen to respond in the same way. Now, the time had come to begin walking it out. *Oh, Lord, help. We need you desperately. We need your strength, your love, and your guidance! GRACE!!*

✌ ✍

Chapter 3

A Rough Start

༚ ༛

Jaime

When I was eight, our family moved from Arizona to Steamboat Springs, a little ski town in Colorado. That meant I immediately went from having many close friends to having none. Steamboat was a rough place to transfer to, especially for a girl in the third grade. It was a small town, with roughly 7,000 residents, and my peers had been in the same class with each other since kindergarten. Not only did I *not* fit in, but they didn't seem to want to get to know me. Needless to say, making friends was extremely difficult.

Although I eventually befriended a few girls who brought me into their circle, the ridiculing and teasing from some other of my peers continued through middle school. Their words and rejection began as scratches on my soul, and over the years those seemingly trivial scratches became deep cuts that wounded my very core.

Just before my freshman year, I asked my parents if I could homeschool the following year as the situation at school had become too much to deal with. That same year, my mother resigned from her position as the choral director at the junior and senior high school, so we had more time together, which brought us closer.

My relationship with the Lord also grew during that time. I had enjoyed a close relationship with Him since I was little, and as a young teenager He started talking to me in dreams and numbers[1] and we developed our own unique "language." Later, I attended several major youth conferences that strengthened my personal relationship with Him.

The summer before my junior year, I decided to return to public school. Although I played volleyball on the high school team and sang in the choir those two years of homeschooling, I missed being around people regularly and felt it was the time to go back and finish school with my class.

My junior year, I returned with new confidence. I didn't care what my peers thought about me and was just there to do my best in school and finish well. People seemed to notice the change in me. I hadn't been the slightest bit popular among my class before, but that year I quickly made more friends, and in the fall of my senior year was nominated for Homecoming Queen.

Although I wasn't crowned, this was the event I recognize as being the beginning of my downfall. I equate it to walking into a deep river. You don't suddenly find yourself chest high in raging rapids you can't escape. It starts with a small step from the shore into the calm, shallow water—a compromise—a decision you make to say or do something you know won't directly result in harm. However, it doesn't stop there. That one step leads to other steps, each one moving you further and further into deeper waters. Soon you find yourself knee high, then waist high; still thinking you're in control and that you can turn around whenever you deem fit. Then, without realizing it, it's too late. You're caught up by a strong current that makes you lose your foothold and the powerful waters swiftly carry you downstream.

So what was my first step into the river? Desiring my peers' approval. For years I had been starved for approval and validation from them and when they started to come around, I wanted more. More approval. More acceptance. Now, I knew I had a relationship with the Lord, knew how to hear His voice, and loved Him dearly. I had parents who loved me and a dad who always showed me the Father's heart. Yet, even with all of that, I put too much emphasis on being liked by people instead of finding my security in *God's* approval of me

Throughout my senior year I found myself making little compromises. I started acting a little more flirtatious with the guys in looks, words and tone of voice, and they responded. *One step.* I started dressing trendier with tighter, more revealing clothes. *Another step.*

It seemed like I was just playing and having fun, but it was actually fire I was playing with. My parents could see it, too. I can't count how many times my mother commented on my choice of attire and I would just shrug her off thinking she just didn't have a clue to what the current fashions were. What I was wearing was just fine. And hey, it's what everyone else was wearing!

I didn't realize how deep the water was until the month before graduation. It was springtime and the senior parties were starting. I had never been one to party and although I had been invited to many before, I had never gone. During my senior year I wasn't exactly making choices consistent with what I believed, but I did know I didn't want to drink. That was my line. But unfortunately, at some point I gave in and crossed it. I was dating a guy who partied, so out of fear of him breaking up with me I started attending them. The first couple of times I refused to drink. Then the inevitable happened and I started—not because I actually liked the taste, but rather out of fear of not fitting in. *A couple more steps.* Ironically enough, one night when I realized his motives weren't pure, I refused and ended the relationship.

I was so proud of myself that I had been able to make the right decision in that moment. I thought I could handle myself with alcohol; that I could stay in control and think rationally under the influence. However, as I continued going to parties and drinking; one beer became two, then four. I was so foolish. So naive to think I could hold onto my godly principles and maintain purity when alcohol flooded my rationale.

Two weeks after graduation I went to a house party with a few friends and some college students I didn't know were there. I let my guard down and drank too much. The next thing I knew, one of the college guys invited me down the hallway to a bedroom. Although things progressed and I kept saying "No…I don't want this…No…," I was too inebriated to stop what was happening.

Afterwards, I got in my car and drove the three miles home—undoubtedly the longest miles I have ever driven. By the grace of God I made it home alive. Crying hysterically, I was in total and utter disbelief that I had lost my virginity to some random college guy whose last name I didn't even know. Although the effects of alcohol were still running through my veins, I knew what this meant, not just for me, but for my parents, my future husband, and most importantly, in the eyes of God. Such intense pain and shame came on me. *How could God forgive me for this?* True, it was to my credit that I said, "No," but I had played a part in this by putting myself in a volatile position.

At the time it seemed I had blown it so badly there was no way to easily escape this river. I was already too far in and to gain a foothold and get out was nearly impossible. Looking back I realize I was still very close to the shore; to turn around would have been simple. But there was a part of me that didn't believe I deserved God's love and forgiveness. Instead of running into the Lord's arms and to my parents for their love and support, I went with the flow and continued down the river, each rapid pulling me under, one after another. It started me on a course headed for disaster. *If I only knew then what I know now.*

A couple of years later, I met an Australian at work who had been in town for the winter. He had many wonderful qualities, not to mention his accent, and we were inseparable from the day we met until he left to head back home. The last time I saw him, he was walking through the security gates at the airport to board his plane. As tears streamed down my face, I watched him disappear into the crowd, and it was then I realized I had fallen in love.

I started feeling nauseous two weeks later and the rest is history. As crazy as it sounds, I *never once* thought that my promiscuity would lead to pregnancy. It *never* crossed my mind. I think I believed the Lord would shield me from getting pregnant; that although I was living in sin, out of His love for me, He would not let that happen.

Looking back I realize it was *because* of His great love for me He *allowed* it to happen. It was my wake-up call; my "Come to Jesus" moment. This was the very thing that got my attention; the very thing that changed my life.

☙ ❧

Chapter 4

Mercy

❧ ☙

Lisa

That night I slept fitfully. Every so often the pain woke me, but too tired to get up, I rolled off the edge of the bed, dropped to the floor on my knees, and wept. I was in the Lord's presence, and that's where I needed to be. Each time, after it subsided, I crawled back into bed for a little bit more sleep.

Jaime called the next morning and asked if I could possibly come home. She said she needed me desperately. As I pondered that question, I thought about my odd situation. For the first time, possibly ever, I was truly stuck—stuck in a situation where I couldn't run to the aid of my child. My heart ached because I wanted so very much to do just that; my arms longed to pull her close and hold her, to hug all the hurt away. But, here I was in the middle of this project with numerous flats of flowers and shrubs to plant, and bags and bags of mulch to spread. Unfortunately, with no one to help for more than just a short amount of time, the responsibility for finishing rested on me and I really couldn't leave until it was completed. I wondered if the Lord had me here alone deliberately. It definitely allowed me to spend a lot more time working this out with Him than I would have spent at home. Perhaps He had a good reason for our temporary separation, giving Jaime time to process it by herself as well.

I told her I was sorry, but I truly could not come home early. I'd be there by the weekend and we could talk by phone every day, as much as she needed. I also reminded her that Daddy loved her very much and was there for her as well.

When Jaime first told me she was pregnant, I realized she was seriously considering having an abortion. It caught me completely off guard. I just assumed we had the same thoughts about this; she would carry the baby and we would all figure the rest out when I got back home. However, that was not the case. She wasn't sure what she was going to do, but abortion was definitely a consideration. Fortunately, a comment from me wasn't necessary. I knew she was aware I was not in favor of it at all. We were, without a doubt, on opposite sides of this coin.

I believe that at the moment of conception, the Spirit of God comes into the new little cell and a baby's life begins. Abortion kills that baby; one too tiny to choose or to object. I thought she believed that, too. I'd seen pictures of embryos as they grew each week; their little hands and feet, ears and nose. I had learned about their brain waves and heartbeat, and other development information. I assumed Jaime had seen or known about them also. I honestly thought once she had some time to talk with Gene and think it through, she'd change her mind.

However, on one of our phone conversations, she told me she had visited a family planning center and had made up her mind. She was going to have an abortion.

I was stunned. In the few seconds it took to catch my breath, I realized whatever I said at this point would just solidify her decision even further. So, I chose not to talk about it too much. Doing the only thing I knew to do, (the best thing by far), I put this whole matter into the Lord's hands and entrusted it to Him.

The next couple of days brought more of the same. Fortunately, my sister and a friend came by and helped me in the yard for a while which made the work go more quickly. But Jaime had requested I not tell anyone so I still had the news and a volcano of emotions bottled inside.

Sometime in the middle of that night, back in that place on the floor with the Lord, I finally ran out of tears and a deep sense of peace settled down over me. I just stayed there, quiet and still, but completely aware of the Lord's presence. After a while, I sensed a nudge to get back into bed and go back to sleep, and so I did.

Just as the sun began to rise, I sensed the Lord ask me what I wanted. Immediately, my heart replied, *I want her to not be pregnant anymore. I don't know how you would do it, but I want her to not be pregnant.*

Can you believe that? The Lord asked me the question of all questions, and my reply was that Jaime not be pregnant anymore! When God asked Solomon that question, he requested wisdom! I've often wondered how I'd reply if I had the chance, and thought I'd answer with something profound and wise like he did. Yet, in an instant, and without much thought, I asked that Jaime not be pregnant! I wasted my one 'wish' on a request as temporary as that!! *Aghhh!*

However, the thought also surprised and energized me. *Wow! This is God Almighty talking here! And I just asked Him to make her not be pregnant anymore!*

But He **is** the God of the impossible…so,…I guess it's possible!

Now how do I act? What do I do?
Lord, how do I proceed?

As I waited for an answer, a thought came to me: *believe* what I'd just asked for. I also sensed I needed to tell Jaime about it. It took a while longer, just listening, but then what to say to her became clear.

I could hardly wait until it was late enough in the morning for me to call her. I wasn't about to tell her all that had happened. Even though she had a pretty neat relationship with the Lord, the world had done a good job of pulling her into its arena lately. At that time, she didn't want to hear too much about God or godly things. I knew I had to choose my words carefully because a wall of separation existed between us; a harsh and hard wall. This decision to have an abortion had put us on opposite sides and I could hear the determination in her voice.

I told her that as I'd been praying for her that morning, I had a strong leading from the Lord for her to go back and have another blood test. She thought the idea was ridiculous because she'd already done it and the results were what they were. Nevertheless, as I reiterated how strongly I believed the sense had come from the Lord, and asked her if she'd do it, "Just for me," she finally agreed.

For the next several hours, I didn't know what to do, how to act or even what to feel inside. I'd never asked for anything so outlandish from the Lord. I'd seen Him do some amazing things in our lives, but not like causing a pregnancy to just, well, disappear! So, I stayed quiet in my heart, pondering Him, His goodness, and His ways.

Later in the day when I was back up in my room, and though still unable to pray any audible words, I found myself with a word to lift up in the silence of my heart. Just one word. But as I got on my knees it welled up within me. *Mercy*. That was all, just *Mercy*. Everything inside me began crying out for God's mercy.

The next day the yard project began to come together. After hours of hard work (and my regular trips upstairs to be with the Lord) I realized I'd be able to finish the work in time to go home on Saturday.

That evening, tired of my room, but needing to be alone, I decided to take a walk. I headed out down the short hill and across the street to the large city park where green grass and tall trees lined both sides of a path beside a creek. Oblivious to the others in the park and a baseball game in the field across the creek, I walked for the longest time, crying, listening, lifting my heart to the Lord and letting Him lead me through a silent conversation.

Spending time alone with Him had become an incredible thing for me, a true place of refuge. It was a place to let the deep feelings inside me well up and spill over, expressing them however I needed to, and then sensing His comfort and love in return. I later realized my not being able to tell anyone our news kept me running back to Him over and over, and it produced deep and powerful results.

However, I wasn't sure quite how to pray. The weight of Jaime's news still crushed me and I simply didn't know what to do with it. I was aware I was reacting very deeply, and seemed stuck there, but did not know why.

Over the last few days my thoughts had run the gamut from the desires I had for my life and for hers, to wondering what I could have done differently. Where did Gene and I as parents go wrong? What more could we have, or should we have done, that might have prevented this? My dreams for her were to have time to grow up, to enjoy a career she loved, to marry a man she adored and to be financially stable before starting a family. Not this.

At some point that evening, my heart's cry turned into audible words enabling me to get things out in front of me and hear with my ears what only my heart had been able to hear previously.

When I got back to my mother's house, I realized I wasn't finished praying and still needed the space and freedom to continue, so I walked back down the hill. I don't know how many times I walked up and back down that hill praying, but I do know something powerful began to happen inside of me. After quite a while, I started walking back and forth in the cul-de-sac, under the streetlights, still praying, my heart still crying out, *Mercy! Mercy! Mercy!*

I sensed waves coming over me. At first they seemed to lap up over my feet, as if I'd walked out on the beach just far enough for them to come up and curl over them, inviting me out farther. Then they grew larger and larger and began crashing over my head and shoulders.

It scared me at first. *That was exactly how I felt with this whole pregnancy situation!* It felt like waves of the sea crashing over me, pounding me, trying to tear me down, rip me off my footing, and carry me out farther to drown me.

Somewhere, in the midst of all of it, a song rose up in my heart, one from Hillsong named "Magnificent." The phrase, "the raging seas that came crashing over me," played over and over again in my mind.

For quite a while, the Lord had me stay there, walking back and forth, sensing those waves, allowing me to cry and pour out to Him all the hurts and grief inside me.

The waves began to cleanse me, washing me first from the inside, and then from the outside. With each one, I could almost see them, no longer pounding and crashing, but now coming to caress and comfort me, taking all the pain with them as they washed back out to sea.

Then the rest of the song came to mind:

> *"Who compares to You?*
> *Who set the stars in their place?*
> *You who calmed the raging seas*
> *That came crashing over me.*
> *Who compares to You?*
> *You, who bring the morning light.*
> *The hope of all the earth*
> *Is rest assured in Your great love.*
>
> *You are magnificent, eternally wonderful, glorious!*
> *Jesus!*
> *No one ever will compare to You.*
> *Jesus!*

*Where the evening fades
You call forth songs of joy.
As the morning wakes
We your children give you praise.*

*You are magnificent, eternally wonderful, glorious!
Jesus!
No one ever will compare to You.
Jesus!"*[2]

The Lord began to reveal them to me as waves of mercy—waves of His great love, His great compassion, undeserved and unreserved. This was the very thing my heart had been crying out for during the last several days. Mercy! And it was being poured out on and in me.

Chapter 5

An Emotional Ride

Lisa

The next morning I received the phone call I'd been expecting. In a rush of emotion Jaime said, "Mother, you're never going to believe this. I'm NOT pregnant! I just heard back about my blood test and I'm am not pregnant!"

The news stunned me for a few seconds. Then incredible relief, the wonder of it all, and all-encompassing gratitude washed over me. While I'd asked the Lord for this, to hear that He'd actually done it floored me!

With renewed energy, I wrapped up the project at my mother's and packed for my flight home the next day.

Saturday afternoon I arrived home, glad to have the rest of the weekend to spend time with Gene and Jaime and process the last several days with one another before we went in different directions on Monday. I hugged Jaime for the longest time and told her how much I loved her. She asked me to forgive her for everything and I told her I had. In a state of shock at all that had just transpired, made even more difficult because we'd been apart, we were relieved the roller coaster week of emotions lay behind us, incredibly thankful for the way it turned out. Talk about *mercy*! We just witnessed God doing the impossible in our lives.

Then came Monday morning…

About 10 a.m., I received another phone call from a very stunned daughter, but unlike the previous one, this call was completely void of emotion. Jaime's doctor's office had called to tell her the blood test had been misread and that she was, indeed, pregnant. Thinking it might be an ectopic pregnancy, they scheduled her for an ultrasound on Thursday to check everything out. She told me she had already made an appointment for an abortion in Denver next week.

Instantly, the roller coaster thundered right back into my life with all of its familiar pain. Shocked and bewildered, because I thought the Lord had answered my prayer, I called Gene to relay the new development, and then went to the Lord in prayer. As before, words failed me, so I just listened. I didn't know what to think. All I knew was that Jaime was pregnant and we were back on the old track, needing answers, needing direction, needing His peace. And abortion?! To me, it was not the solution, but I wasn't sure how to proceed with that either, so I just stayed quiet, listening for His direction.

Later that day I remembered something a friend told me a month prior when we "happened" to run into her and her husband at the River Walk in San Antonio. I knew it was a divine appointment—a God thing—but at the time I didn't know why. While visiting family in Texas, we wanted to see The Alamo and a few other well-known sites in San Antonio. As we walked down the River Walk, we noticed the couple ahead of us looked much like friends who had led the home fellowship we attended in Arizona years ago. When we called out to them, *"Julie, Bruce?,"* they turned around, and sure enough, we were right.

We spent an hour or so catching up on family and old friends, and during that time, Julie mentioned that Kathy, a mutual friend, would soon become a grandmother. Her son and his girlfriend were expecting and the baby was due soon. She suggested I call her, but I'd forgotten about it and hadn't done it yet. I had a strong feeling that phone call was my next step. I knew we would need strong support and godly counsel to get through all of this.

When I reached her, Kathy responded graciously with love and compassion. She told me their story and let me ask questions and then stated that, most importantly, we needed to allow Jaime to make this decision herself, with no pressure. She reminded me, "This is her life, not yours, and she will have to live the rest of her life with every decision she makes." She stressed the importance of loving and supporting her unconditionally, regardless of her decision and all the decisions that would come later, even if we didn't agree. "Jaime needs to know that nothing she has done or will ever do will change your love for her."

She also suggested I print off a brochure from a website she gave me on unplanned pregnancies. She told me it would help to give it to Jaime with any other information that would enable her to make a good, informed decision. She said too often family planning centers and well-meaning friends give partial or inaccurate information that may persuade girls to "get it over with," and "get on with" their life. However, it's not until afterward that they experience the physical, emotional and spiritual repercussions, and then have to live with them as well as terrible regrets.

She reminded me of God's presence right there with us, leading and directing us, and encouraged me to trust Him with each step; to place it all in His hands and let Him do His work.

Gratitude filled me as I thought about His directing me to make that phone call. It turned out to be a huge blessing. This dear friend had given me love, encouragement and support, not condemnation or shame, in addition to some sound advice and direction.

I found the website[3] and printed the brochure. It was excellent. In an unbiased and educational format, it explained all the options for an unplanned pregnancy:

- Carrying the baby and parenting it (with suggestions).
- Carrying the baby and placing it for adoption (with a few options).
- Having an abortion (with a long list of risks and possible long lasting negative physical, emotional and spiritual effects. Also included were questions geared to help the mother decide if she were strong enough physically and emotionally to have the procedure done, and remain healthy in the months and years to come.)

As Gene and I read these lists, we saw things we had never considered. First, we'd not even thought about adoption. What a great option! A little life is spared and a couple's heart's desire for a baby fulfilled. Second, up to this point, when the subject of abortion arose, we had just thought of the baby. Now, suddenly, our concerns included the mother—Jaime! The list of risks and long lasting negative effects shocked us, and we suspected that no one from the family planning center, or anyone else, for that matter, had talked to her about any of them. We desperately wanted her to be spared the consequences listed there, as well as the hurt and shame she was already experiencing.

As we discussed these things, we both admitted with some embarrassment that we had thought about abortion as a possible option in the last several days. However, having worked through those thoughts, we came back to our original decision on this issue, made several years ago. We truly believed our conviction that God breathes life into the embryo the moment of conception and a baby's life begins. Abortion takes the life of that unborn child.

As it turned out, the brochure we printed in hopes of changing Jaime's mind strengthened our resolve, and for that we were both thankful.

Gene and I prayed constantly, continually putting the situation into the Lord's hands. We knew anything we said might pressure her to take the matter into her own hands and run with her decision, without paying attention to His direction for her. We absolutely trusted Him to direct her along the best path for her. We hoped with all our hearts her decision would include life for her baby and not abortion. We also prayed the Lord would prepare her heart regarding the brochure, and that I would choose my words well, presenting them gently enough that she would, indeed, read it.

Soon afterwards, the Lord opened a door of opportunity enabling me to introduce the subject and give Jaime the brochure. However, the considerable tension between us made the conversation difficult. I proceeded as carefully and tenderly as possible and told her about it; that it was good and informative, speaking to all the options, including one I hadn't even thought of before, adoption. Also that it included some information on abortion I hadn't known, but thought would interest her as she made her decision.

"Daddy and I realize this is your life and, therefore, your decision to make." Then I said to her very deliberately, "We know you know how to hear from God, and we believe He will lead you to the perfect answer for this situation, and He will lead you *through* it." Conscious God had me *declare* those words to her, I believed with all my heart He would do what the scripture in Job states: "You will declare a thing and it will be established for you."[4] With all my heart I trusted Him to plant those words deep in her heart, and that they *would* produce good fruit!

Finally, I told her we loved her very much, were praying for her, and would support whatever decision she made.

Chapter 6

Letting Go

Lisa

I didn't realize how hard it would be for me to say that...and *mean* it! In that last statement, I truly let go. I realized I didn't like it. Not one little bit! In all honesty, I wanted to stay in there and say and do things that would make her decide to go *my* way. But I knew she had to be free from me, from Gene, and from all the pressure so she could hear God and follow Him. I knew that He, and He alone, knew *her*, her future, and the plans He had for her. And, I knew I had to truly let go, and then trust Him with all my might.

It wasn't new for us. Gene and I'd done it off and on over our lifetimes. It's an incredible way to live, and can be scary at first. But the Lord is absolutely amazing, and so very faithful. His love for us is so wonderful, so deep, and so all-encompassing. Something we can (and need to) completely trust. However, knowing that doesn't make it easy.

When Jaime left for college a couple of years before, we had to let go and it proved to be extremely difficult for me. She had been a great student, responsible and not really interested in partying, but something had happened early in the summer and she'd changed. Somewhere along the line she got drawn into that scene and with her new freedom and independence at college, things were different.

She became distant, not wanting much of a relationship with us and seemingly not interested in the Lord, either. Fortunately she had given her life to Him when she was little and had seen the amazing things He had done in our lives, and in hers. He had spoken to her powerfully through dreams, visions, and prophetic words, and I believed she would hold onto Him in the long run.

Even so, I had a continual knot in my stomach with worry I simply could not shake. I began to sense God encouraging me to let go and put her in His hands; then to trust Him. He showed me that at this point in her life, there was nothing more I could do or say that would make a difference. My part now was to love her, pray for her, and trust Him with all of my heart to take care of her, lead her, and fill in all the gaps in her life.

During that time, fear gnawed at me constantly. It frightened me to think about her life at college, knowing what might be going on, and yet realizing I had absolutely no power to do anything but to trust God. (I know, silly thought. After all, He *is* God *Almighty!*) But He led me to be aggressive about that trust. Each time fear tried to enter my mind, I made a deliberate decision to stop it immediately, and then, consciously entrust Jaime to Him. As often as I could, I said out loud and rather violently, *"No, I will **not** be afraid! Lord, I put her in Your hands. I **trust You** with her life!"* And in situations where I could not say it out loud, I'd pray it quietly under my breath.

The warfare I waged was for both Jaime and me—leaving her in the Lords hands, keeping her there, not taking her back to worry over her, forbidding fear to have its way, and finally declaring my trust and dependence in the Lord. At first, I prayed it almost moment by moment each time the fear crept in. After a while, it occurred only every five minutes, then ten, then every hour or two. Then, it happened only occasionally during the day, and eventually only a time or two each week. However, the exertion it required paid off. I slowly made headway with that fear, confronting and refusing its entrance, giving it to the Lord and making room for His peace to take over.

Gene is able to let go easily, but I have a more difficult time with it. However, when I do let go, my trust in Him is strengthened, reinforcing my ability to do it the next time. God doesn't always let me see the results immediately, but I've watched Him turn things around several times.

One of these times was at the end of Jaime's first year of college. Something had been stirring inside me and I felt led to ask Him, if He did not want her to go back to college the next year, would He change her mind? The day she left school to drive home for the summer, she told me in a phone call she could hardly wait to get back to school for the fall semester. However, when she arrived the next day, before unloading a single thing from her car, she walked right into the house, called my name, ran upstairs to find me, and said there was something she needed to tell me.

"Mother, on the drive home the Lord told me He didn't want me to go back this fall. I hope that's okay with you, because I feel I'm not supposed to go."

> *Trust in the Lord with all your heart and do not lean on your own understanding;*
> *Acknowledge Him in all your ways, knowing and believing that He will make your path straight.*
> *(Proverbs 3:5-6)[5]*

Chapter 7

Turning Point

Lisa

Jaime asked me to go with her to the ultrasound appointment, and I agreed, but oh, I did not want to be there. Like her, I hated having to walk this journey. I kept wanting out; to be able to quit and just get back to normal life. But there was no way out. The only way out was to go through it. She'd already experienced so much and I didn't want her to have to face this alone. She needed me to be there with her and I could certainly be strong and be by her side. Still, the thought of her being pregnant and knowing all that was to come added to the huge knot in my stomach.

As we waited in the cold exam room, I realized she'd already been through this before: waiting, wondering, being fearful. My heart ached for her.

Jaime

That day, May 23, turned out to be the pivotal point of my life. I was grateful my mother agreed to be there with me as we sat in the exam room waiting patiently for the nurse to come in and perform the ultrasound. I was extremely nervous. Since the blood test results were inconclusive, I wasn't sure what the outcome of the ultrasound would be. At this point, I had to be ready for anything, though what did happen, and my response, took me completely by surprise.

The technician moved the ultrasound wand as we watched the monitor and listened to the ambient swishing sounds. Suddenly we heard a different, more distinct sound and she turned to me and said calmly, "There you go. That's your baby's heartbeat."

I froze. On the monitor in front of me was a tiny spot pulsating in perfect harmony with the heartbeat coming from the speakers. In an instant everything in me changed. I looked up at my mother. Even though the technician continued talking, explaining the picture on the screen and that everything looked normal, I didn't hear a word of it. As I sat there, watching the heartbeat of this life inside of me, the miraculous reality of it being a person was overwhelming. In a moment, my fears evaporated and were replaced with excitement and hope. As soon as she left the room, I said, "Mom! That was a heartbeat, not just a mass of cells. It is a *baby*! And it's up to me to protect it!"

I knew what I had to do. Although I was only six weeks along, this was clearly not a cluster of cells, but a *life*. I had heard and seen my baby's heartbeat. And I knew God was entrusting me with the responsibility of protecting and caring for this life…*my baby*. I didn't know how it would all work out nor did I have any answers at this point. What I did know was the Lord would not ask me to walk through anything without giving me the grace and tools to do it. It was obvious what He was asking of me, and at that moment I decided to accept it wholeheartedly and put my trust in Him to lead me. I could not do this without Him, nor did I want to.

Lisa

As soon as the door shut, Jaime began talking excitedly about what had just happened. Emotions tossed back and forth inside my heart. I was grateful there was a baby's heartbeat to be heard and that she immediately embraced being pregnant, but also stunned to realize she'd been told the baby was just a mass of cells. I had no idea she believed it. We could easily have talked through all of that, but I simply didn't know. She hadn't shared those kinds of thoughts with me.

I breathed a long sigh of relief pondering all that had transpired, wondering about what was now to come. *Oh, Lord, thank you. That was amazing…You are amazing.* In that one instant, when we heard her baby's heartbeat, everything changed! The answer to my prayers came just that fast, in the twinkling of an eye.

But it wasn't really in the "twinkling of an eye." It had been coming for several days and I suddenly realized what started this "first she's pregnant…then she isn't…then she is again" thing. It was my seemingly ridiculous request of the Lord for Jaime to not be pregnant that created the delays postponing an abortion until the baby was old enough for Jaime to hear its heartbeat.

Oh, Lord! You knew she would immediately rise to the occasion and take charge…of herself, the situation and the baby growing inside her. You knew how to reach her and how to touch her heart. You took my crazy request and used it. You stretched out the timing until she could realize she was really carrying a baby—her baby!

God's thoughts *are* so much higher than ours.[6] How He even got me to pray that, and then how He took it and changed *everything* dumbfounded me. I thought I had wasted my "wish," but in God's eyes, it was perfect. It changed things! It saved a life! He had an entirely different plan than just having her not be pregnant. She would probably have just gone right back to her old life. But, now? I sensed things would be very different.

The next few days blurred together as we found ourselves in a bit of shock—not that we weren't before—but this was a different kind of shock to be sure. A baby on the way meant all kinds of things to discuss and decisions to make. How were we going to do this? Would Jaime work? Would she and the baby live with us? How were we going to pay for this? What about the father? Would he help out in any way? What about his parents? Questions, questions, questions.

I didn't even get around to thinking about whether she would keep the baby and raise it or place it, but Jaime had. She had already changed gears and was beginning to take charge. She began to eat more nutritiously and make good decisions about her activities and her rest and was more focused and determined.

She told us she didn't want to stay in town through her pregnancy. We lived in a small town and she felt strongly that she needed to go somewhere else. I started checking out options by making phone calls, gathering information, and getting recommendations. Most places turned out to be institutions of one kind or another, most of which were costly and used behavioral modification programs. I was not at all interested in having Jaime go to an institution, (that felt like imprisonment to me), and she would hate it.

I was also adamant about her not going into a program using behavior modification. I don't believe it's effective for permanent change. In my estimation, the only real and lasting change comes from God, His unconditional love, the power of the Holy Spirit, hearing and being in the scriptures, hearing Him, and praising and worshipping Him on a regular basis.

What I hoped for, and silently asked the Lord for, was a safe place, a good place for my daughter to go. I wanted a place with a strong Christian influence and grace, not legalism, and certainly not "religion"—rules and regulations. A place for her to be loved and accepted, where she would receive guidance and healing while she awaited the birth of her baby.

Chapter 8

A Divine Appointment

ಹೇ ಈ

Lisa

In the midst of this whirlwind, dear friends invited us for dinner. Jill, expecting her third child with only a few weeks to go, was very pregnant and I imagined seeing her so large made it difficult for Jaime. Off and on throughout the evening, my heart turned to her, hurting for her, wondering how she was doing and what her thoughts were. Was she thinking that's how she'd look in several months, possibly agonizing about how she'd do this? Jill and her husband, Brent, didn't know, so we couldn't talk about it at all, which left Jaime alone with her thoughts.

After dinner, they received a phone call from close friends in Nashville and asked if we minded if they took the call. We didn't mind, and spent the time visiting among ourselves while they talked. Later they explained the situation. Their friends were adopting a baby through Mercy Ministries, a Christian ministry and residential home for girls in crisis in Nashville. The young mother had just given birth, but wanted to change her mind and keep the baby. Upset, they called for support and prayer. (Later, we heard the mother followed through with her original decision and placed her baby with them.)

They went on to tell us about Mercy Ministries and their high regard for it. Supporters for years, and impressed with how it was run, they said the fruit was amazing. They described it as first-class in every way. Sustained by donations and contributions, not state or federal funds, it was free to be run as a Christian ministry. All the young women accepted into the program attended without any cost to them or their families. It was absolutely free.

Years ago, Nancy Alcorn, the founder of Mercy Ministries, spent several years working for a state-run correctional facility for delinquent juvenile girls. Having investigated child abuse cases, she had "direct encounters with secular programs that were not producing permanent results demonstrating changed lives."[7] She saw many of the girls leave or be forced out of the system having used all their insurance and personal money and being sent home with no true and permanent life change. Many ended up in the "women's prison system because they never got the real help they needed." She recognized that "real transformation would never come as the result of any government system" and that "only Jesus could bring restoration into the lives of girls who were desperately hurting...."[8] She cried out to God for a better way.

As she prayed, God unfolded the plan that became Mercy Ministries. It consisted of a program designed to take the girls in and protect them from the influences of their previous lives, saturate them in the unconditional love of God through the Word, praise and worship, and teach them how to live healthy, successful lives in the power of the Holy Spirit.

Our friends explained the girls had daily Bible study, praise and worship, and teaching sessions, as well as individual and group counseling and times of prayer. The pregnant girls took decision-making classes designed to give them enough information to help them in their decisions whether to place their babies for adoption or to parent them, and classes to help them walk out those decisions. Because of the calm and steady atmosphere created in the home, they had heard it claimed that "Mercy babies" were born calmer and healthier than others.

Then they described the home itself. The spacious building, on a large property in Nashville, included a large commercial kitchen, two large dining rooms, a sizeable family room with big-screen TV, and spacious classrooms and offices. With two girls to a bedroom and every two bedrooms sharing an adjoining bathroom, the home housed 40 girls. They described it as beautifully decorated, intentionally designed to make a physical demonstration of God's unconditional love to the girls who came to live there.

Brent and Jill spoke passionately as they talked about "Mercy," and we spoke for a long time about it. They told several stories of people they knew who had gone through Mercy themselves, or who knew others who had gone through the program there. Every story was remarkable.

Curiosity rose in me. Was this our answer? It had come so easily! These friends didn't know about Jaime's pregnancy, and they usually didn't answer a phone call in the middle of a visit. This whole thing struck me as uncanny, but so like God. The evening had His fingerprints all over it.

I knew better than to show anything more than a casual interest in Mercy Ministries to Jaime because it might make her back off, so I decided to wait and let Gene bring it up. After we got home, he asked her what she thought about Brent and Jill's comments. We talked casually about it for a few minutes and then she responded, saying she simply didn't think it was for her, and went to bed. Gene and I talked about it a bit more and prayed about it together and, once again, placed the whole matter into God's hands.

The next morning I looked up Mercy Ministries on the internet. The website described it as a "free-of-charge, voluntary, faith-based residential program that serves young women from all socio-economic backgrounds ages 13-28 who face a combination of life-controlling issues such as eating disorders, self-harm, drug and alcohol addictions, depression, and unplanned pregnancy. Mercy also serves young women who have been physically and sexually abused..."[9] Nothing like a "home" I had imagined and definitely not an institution; it looked more like a beautiful dormitory on the grounds of a well-kept college campus. Everything was beautiful and spacious just as Brent and Jill had described.

The ministry had established a structured program, and the girls coming in knew they could expect to be there for about six months. Every morning after a scheduled time of individual Bible reading and prayer, the girls began their chores. Daily and weekly rotating schedules included cleaning, dusting, and vacuuming the bathrooms, halls, and bedrooms, etc., as well as preparing and cooking the meals and cleaning up afterwards.

After breakfast the girls spent time in praise and worship, followed by some form of Christian teaching, either through DVDs or a speaker. Then, back to meal preparation and cleanup. After lunch the girls attending school had a classroom in which they did their schoolwork while the others received guidance in the form of individual and group counseling sessions. The schedule included a little down time and then preparations for dinner and cleanup.

The evenings held more praise, worship, and teaching, followed by personal time for reading and counseling assignments; and then lights out.

The weekly schedule included a couple of afternoons exercising at the YMCA and some shopping time for a few hours every Friday afternoon for the girls' personal needs at either Target or the mall. Each Sunday morning and Wednesday evening they went as a group to church.

To be honest, I wondered if it were too strict, too rigid, and perhaps even legalistic. Jaime and I visited a Christian college like that a few years before, and disliked the environment immensely. If a similar atmosphere cloaked this ministry, Jaime would not do well here. However, I understood the reasoning for it all. To have a chance for change, the girls' old way of life (music, books, and movies, etc.), and old relationships (friends, boyfriends and even family), had to be kept to a minimum so good, healthy, and godly habits could begin to take root.

I couldn't tell, but our friends weren't the legalistic type and had nothing but rave reviews about it. I needed to research this aspect of Mercy Ministries more.

When I saw Jaime later that morning, I casually told her I'd gone online to check out Mercy Ministries and told her a little bit about what I'd found. I gave her the website address and told her she might be interested to see what it said. She told us she'd been thinking about it and wondered if I'd go with her to meet with our friends again, let them know about her situation, and find out more about it.

Jaime and I met with Jill, while Gene met separately with Brent. Both responded to our news lovingly and with great compassion and asked how they could help us, which meant the world to us. They answered our concerns about the rules and possible legalism and assured us that an overwhelming sense of unconditional love filled the home. Mercy Ministries aspired to demonstrate to the girls from the beginning, in every way they could, they were special and very much loved. The rules were established to maximize the change in the girls' lives, to protect them, and to help them move as far along as possible during their stay.

Brent and Jill also shared that Joyce Meyer was one of the main teachers through her DVDs. An avid fan and supporter of Mercy Ministries, she had donated a great deal of her materials to them. I was grateful to hear that, because Joyce is a good, strong, balanced Bible teacher, easy to listen to, and she teaches a doctrine of grace. In fact, I had contacted Joyce Meyer Ministries[10] earlier while researching possible places for Jaime to go, and they told me they referred everyone to Mercy Ministries. All this information continued to provide confirmation for me.

The final kicker came when Jill said, *"Oh, you already know all this! You've been there!"*

"What!?..."

Yes, five years before, Jaime had been on tour with Young Continentals, a Christian singing group that performed at Mercy Ministries in Nashville. I flew in and stayed with Brent and Jill so I could see her perform. We had been inside the very place we were now considering!

Then Jaime remembered something else, incredibly ironic now, from that performance. During one of the songs about Jesus being able to help in any situation, that no circumstance was beyond His control, she actually played the part of a young pregnant girl who turned to Him.

Hearing this absolutely floored me. Once again, God's goodness and His incredible love for us overwhelmed me. If Mercy Ministries was the answer He had for Jaime, he had truly gone before us and made a way. Even five years before we needed the answer, He had prepared a place for her, knowing what she would need. And He led us right to it.

Mercy wasn't just the deep love and compassion of God, or even just the undeserved favor of God, but now, it was also a literal dwelling place provided for her. *Exactly* the kind of place I had asked the Lord for.

I didn't know for certain Jaime would choose Mercy Ministries. We talked about it on the way home. Jaime wasn't completely convinced, but our conversation with Jill encouraged both of us a great deal.

☙ ❧

Jaime

I wasn't sure what I thought about Mercy Ministries. I felt it was most likely the Lord's leading as He orchestrated me visiting the home a few years before, but the strict schedule made me very apprehensive. I didn't think I would do well with such structure as, quite frankly, I liked being free to set my own schedule. I had lived on my own for almost two years and had grown accustomed to not having someone watch over my shoulder, making sure my chores were done on a regular basis and that I went to bed at a decent hour. So to go from such freedom to an environment with hardly any at all made me considerably nervous.

If I were going to go, I was the one who needed to make that decision. If I felt it was more my parents' decision than my own, I knew I wouldn't have the resolve to stay in the program and finish well when things became challenging, as I expected they would. Although I loved the sound of the decision-making class and that they had an in-house adoption agency, I wouldn't just be going for the baby. This was a comprehensive program that would address my deeper issues, and I had a feeling the time there wouldn't be all sunshine and roses. Hard days would come. Days when I would want nothing more than to walk out of those doors and head straight home. But if I decided to go, I would be there until I graduated. Failure was not an option.

I spent a lot of time in prayer those next couple of days. I knew the Lord had a plan for my life and the baby's, but was Mercy it? This was such a big and important decision. *Please don't let me miss it, Lord!* I made myself get really quiet and still as I rested on my bed, curled up with a fluffy pillow. In that moment, I couldn't help but feel an overwhelming sense of peace about Mercy. Yes, this was where I felt the Lord was leading me—from the divine appointment with Brent and Jill to the discovery that I had been in the Nashville home years before. I decided I would apply and I believed if the Lord was in it, I would be accepted. If not, He would guide me down another path. But I had to walk down this one first to see where it led.

Lisa

A day or two later, Jaime came to us and said she'd spent a great deal of time praying about Mercy and believed God was, indeed, leading her to go there. She had already called and talked with them, had gotten more information, and had downloaded an application. Although quite lengthy, she wanted to work on it and get it into the mail the next day.

She said that unless God was in it, she wouldn't get accepted. She'd learned there were 400 girls on the waiting list and only two Mercy homes in the U.S, one in Monroe, Louisiana and the one in Nashville. (Now there are four homes in the U.S., with international affiliates in several countries and more in the planning stages.) The Nashville home, the larger of the two, housed 40 girls, but had only a few openings. The staff prayed over each application, seeking God's guidance for wisdom in the process. But she said she believed it was exactly where God was leading her, and so did we, so we sat down and prayed over the application and the whole situation, then put it into God's hands.

You can imagine how waiting for their response challenged our patience over those next days. With the baby's due date in early January, Jaime was already into her second month of pregnancy. She really wanted to be re-situated by the time she started showing, so our time was growing short.

If Mercy didn't accept her, we didn't know what we were going to do. We saw no other decent options. However, even though we'd put all of our eggs into one basket, that's where we believed God had led us, and we just had to wait until we heard back from them.

A week or two later, Jaime received the call. One of the staff members told her they had prayed about it in their meeting and believed the Lord wanted her there, and so did they. She asked Jaime if she still wanted to come. When she said, *"Yes, of course!"* they welcomed her and told her they'd see her at 2 p.m., August 8.

Just like that! In just a minute or two we had a plan…a wonderful plan. All the pieces, all the circumstances, all the uncertainty came together in a moment. It was one of those "suddenlies" you read about in the Word and trust God for. But when they come, they still surprise you. They catch you off guard and stun you for a moment. Then God's love and mercy and grace flood you like a big gentle wave, filling you, saturating every cell, every fiber, and every part of your being, and you find yourself in complete amazement at Him and His marvelous ways.

Jaime and I just stood there looking at each other for a moment, taking it all in. Then the relief and gratitude for what God had just done washed over us and we hugged each other, laughing and thanking Him.

God is our refuge and strength,
a very present help in trouble.[11]
(Psalms 46:1 NKJ)

Chapter 9

Mercy Ministries

⊱ ⊰

Lisa

August 8 (8/8) at 2 p.m. was the date and time scheduled for Jaime to enter Mercy Ministries. We immediately recognized its significance, and knew it was good, very good. I knew without a shadow of a doubt this was more than it appeared on the surface. God had provided a divine appointment for Jaime that would mark the beginning of a new life for her.

Several years before, I had attended a fascinating Bible study on the meaning of numbers in scripture. I had no idea God used numbers (and colors and the meaning of names, etc.) to give more insight into the scriptures, Himself, and His love and purposes for us. It astonished me to see it proved over and over again, scripture after scripture. How like Him to use various ways and layers of understanding to speak to us, to love and encourage us, to delight us, and to let us know He is right there with us. He loves hiding these little nuggets right there in the Word, in our lives, and in nature for us to find—something like a divine treasure hunt. And when we notice them, we end up enjoying Him, trusting Him more, and loving Him more. It becomes a wonderful cycle as our awareness of Him and His involvement in every area of our lives blossoms.

I shared the teaching with Gene and the family and we began noticing the numbers here and there. At first we thought they were uncanny little coincidences. However, as time passed and we became more conscious of them, we realized they were more than that; God was speaking to us through them.

I made a list of the meanings of several of the numbers and kept it in the back of my Bible, and checked from time to time, to see if they pertained to our circumstances. Some of them didn't, however quite a few did, and over the last number of years the Lord has used them repeatedly.

Many know the number 7 in scripture signifies completion, perfection, or rest, but the meanings of some other numbers are not as well-known:

2 - Separation.

3 - Refers to the third day of Jesus, which speaks of all that happened on the day of His resurrection: supernatural power, miracles, life, and the purpose of God.

5 - Refers to grace, divine blessing, unearned and undeserved favor, loving-kindness, God's mercy, the empowerment of the Holy Spirit, or 'God's Riches at Christ's Expense'. (The Lord seems to emphasize the empowerment of the Holy Spirit as He speaks through these numbers to us.)

8 - New beginnings.

9 - Completion of the time of pregnancy; the time it takes to bring a thing to birth.

In Jaime's life, the Lord used and continues to use the number 5 (grace) frequently, almost to the point of absurdity. However, it caught our attention and we now understand He's letting us know He's here, very involved in our lives, with very specific purposes; blessing us and giving us His power for what's ahead.

So, in the midst of these difficult times, when the numbers 2 (separation)—the time of her Mercy Ministry admissions appointment; and 8 (new beginnings)—the month and day of that appointment appeared, it was significant. In the number 2, God revealed a separation was coming, dividing Jaime's past from all that was to come. In the number 8, He assured us He was right there with us in all of this, He would give her His strength to walk this journey and Mercy Ministries was indeed the path He had chosen for her. It would be a great new beginning!

From where we stood, here in late June, August 8 seemed an eternity away. I wished, for several reasons, Jaime could go earlier. She wanted to be away from home before she started showing, and I wanted that for her, too. I could only imagine how difficult it all was as she didn't talk about her feelings much, keeping most of her thoughts to herself. I also wanted her to start the program at Mercy Ministries and begin to move through all the decisions I knew she'd need to make.

There wasn't much we could do while we waited for August to come. We made a good attempt at taking advantage of the time that remained and tried to enjoy some of our summer as a family here in the beautiful Colorado mountains. Gene planned a camping trip for us up into a remote area and we fished and hiked, roasting marshmallows by the campfire each evening. On another outing we rode our horses on trails through shimmering aspen groves while our dog, Zip, ran alongside.

As the eighth of August drew near, we helped where we could as Jaime sorted through her things, deciding what to take. She didn't need maternity clothes yet, so we decided to purchase them later. Even though she would have a closet of her own, a tall dresser, a nightstand and some room in the bathroom for toiletries, etc., everything she needed for the next six months or so had to fit in there.

Finally the day came for us to pack up the car and make the drive from Colorado to Nashville. It was two long days in the car together and none of us felt like making conversation. I bought ginger candy to help with Jaime's inevitable car sickness, snacks and a couple of books on CD to help pass the time.

Even though no one spoke about it, we were all still a bit apprehensive about Mercy, despite the wonderful reports we'd heard. You don't really know about a place until you get there and experience it in person. And though Jaime was making this decision herself, it still felt as if we were the ones about to commit our daughter to this place for the minimum six months.

It was a little unnerving. Did we know enough about it? Was it a truly safe place? Everyone we had spoken to thought so. Even so, I had to remind myself Jaime was now twenty years old. This was her life and, like us, she was trusting God to lead her and to be with her.

I don't know exactly what was going on, but I could not get my mind to see down the road. Even though God had worked everything out so far and all the reports of Mercy amazed us, it never occurred to me that one day all of this would end. It would all work out and she would either be a single mother living with us or somewhere else, or the baby would be adopted and she'd be trusting God to lead her into the next season of her life. Oddly enough, none of it occurred to me. The only thing I could see was the step I was currently taking and a little of the one that would come immediately after that. I knew God would continue to lead us with every step, every decision, and every situation and we trusted Him with our whole hearts. He would provide the strength and fortitude we needed to walk it all out.

Thank heavens we had Him to lead us and open up a way! What in the world do people do who don't have Him…who don't know Him?

As we drove up the driveway, past the large Mercy Ministries sign at the entrance to the property, I noticed how beautiful everything was; so incredibly green. A huge, well-cared-for lawn and tall leafy trees invited us up towards the sprawling home. Neither our previous visit, nor the pictures we had seen prepared me for the welcoming and serene atmosphere. As we parked the car and walked down the sidewalk to the front doors, my heart tightened into a hard knot. Here we were at the place God had so supernaturally provided. I should have been excited—or something—but I only felt numb.

We walked through the large front doors into the lobby and peered into the spacious living room. The hallways off the lobby to each side were vacant, but Christian music played softly and I noticed I was beginning to relax. A young woman welcomed us and asked us to wait a few minutes while she let "Mamma Boo" know we were here.

Mamma Boo! Something deep inside me smiled. Her name, along with the peace that practically oozed out of the walls, began to do its work on me. This certainly wasn't going to be a hard place in which to live. I remembered Brent and Jill had said Mercy believed in showing the girls the unconditional love of God in every way they could, even in the decor of the home. They obviously meant it. Mercy was lovely.

As we waited, we looked at the pictures on the wall and Jaime and I talked about how much nicer this was than we had remembered. Then another young woman came out of the office, introduced herself, and offered to give us the tour.

The layout of the home impressed us; the bedrooms and adjoining bathrooms, the large commercial kitchen, laundry room, classrooms, counseling offices, etc. Not only was it spacious and beautiful, but it was immaculate. And, as I continually noted, so very peaceful.

Within a few minutes we were ushered into Mamma Boo's office, the woman who would explain everything to us and get Jaime registered. A large woman with a warm smile and a twinkle in her eye greeted us. She introduced herself and told us how glad everyone was to have Jaime join them. I could feel our fears melt away as she explained the intake process, the daily and weekly schedules, the rules, etc. Everything had its reason and carefully-thought-out purpose. I could tell this was a first-class place, like we'd been told, from the decor to the staff to the rules—everything. I grew more and more impressed and grateful.

She answered our questions and treated us kindly and compassionately, with just the right touch of humor. I knew the girls and the staff, alike, must adore her. *What a blessing for these girls—and now, my girl—to have this wonderful woman with such a motherly love in their lives!*

For the next step of Jaime's admission into Mercy, we brought all her belongings from the car into a room near the office to have them checked in. As we carried them in, I caught myself thinking about how little she had, and that it would be all she would live with for the next six months or so. I was surprised to see the room already filled with other suitcases, pillows and bags, etc. and realized several others must have checked in just before us. We pushed aside a few things and made a pile out of Jaime's belongings when another young woman, a staff member, joined us.

She introduced herself and explained that she and Jaime needed to check her things in. She motioned to the floor and Jaime sat in the middle of her belongings and they began listing everything she had brought with her to Mercy; *every single item...one at a time*!

Gene and I looked for a place to stand and then made our way, gingerly stepping over the piles, to a spot in the corner. I was staring blindly, lost in thought, as we watched this tedious process, when suddenly, we were invited to leave. Another staff member came in and explained it would take a while for them to complete the check in, and Jaime's roommate and a few of the girls would help her move her things into her room. It would probably be better if we left so she could finish the intake and begin to make the transition into being here at Mercy.

That was it! She was here and moving in...not only into the home, but into the next several months of her life! With Mercy now taking her under their wing, our part had abruptly come to an end.

It took several seconds for my mind to grasp what she had said. It simply *did not compute*. It happened so quickly! I don't know that I ever thought about what would happen next. I must have assumed we'd have some time together to say our goodbyes and for Gene and

I to tell Jaime how much we loved her, were proud of her and would be praying for her. I thought perhaps we would be helping her move into her room and settle in. So taken by surprise, I couldn't get my mind to clear and come into the present. I felt as if I were swimming in some unseen substance. The room wasn't real. The conversation wasn't real. Nothing seemed real.

I desperately wanted to have a little time to talk by ourselves, to see how she was doing, to have some closure and then to look forward with expectation to the next part.

But, it didn't happen that way.

I finally asked if we could have a few minutes with her and we carefully found our way back over all the piles of things into the hallway. We started to talk there, but realized we needed to have some privacy, so we moved just outside the main doors. There, we did have a quick prayer together, hugged and told one another we loved each other, and told Jaime how proud of her we were, and then *"poof"*... it was over.

I barely made it to the car before the tears began to flow. Perhaps the progression of things and the swift goodbye was part of Mercy's normal operating procedure. Perhaps they knew, from countless other goodbyes, it was the best for all involved. But it stunned us. It literally took our breath away.

We knew she was an adult, but even so, as our daughter, we felt her fears and uncertainties about the days to come. Now that she was moving into Mercy we wouldn't have much contact with her. Our phone calls and visits would be very restricted. She'd be on her own as far as family was concerned, dealing with everything that comes with being pregnant and not married. She would face the guilt and shame and fears of all kinds without us. She'd walk into those days seeing her stomach grow, feeling the life inside, making decisions, and pressing through this part of her life largely without us. *Would she find friendships? Would she receive the support she needed? Was she going to be okay?* All these, and other thoughts seeped in and out of our minds for the next several hours and days.

Hours later we stopped for the night and settled into our hotel room. As Gene sat down on the bed, he finally broke. It was one of the few times I'd ever seen him cry, and honestly, it helped me tremendously to have him sobbing and praying with me, sharing the pain, the grief, and all that we'd shouldered so far. I think we had been so busy sustaining life, we hadn't taken time to share our thoughts or our feelings. He told me later he felt it had been his job to be strong, to stay in control, to get us through everything for the last three months, and then get us through the long, two-day drive to get to Mercy on time.

He spoke my own heart as he described how, suddenly, there was nothing more he could do for her, and it left him feeling so helpless. Someone else was going to be doing his job—teaching her, helping her, guiding her. He wouldn't really have any direct influence in her life while she was going through this season of her life. With everything now out of his hands, the finality of it set in. It was as if she were gone.

Until then, he had always been there for her when she needed him. That's what fathers do. Now she was on her own, and it felt horrible, as if he weren't there at all.

Chapter 10

Embracing Change

☙ ❧

Jaime

So there I was. My parents had just left and I found myself in a home with 39 other girls and several staff, none of whom I knew. To say I felt nervous is a complete understatement. I had no idea what the days, weeks and months ahead would look like, if I would make friends easily, or how long it would take to get settled in and comfortable in my new surroundings. Being a "planner", I always liked to look ahead and know what to expect, which made this transition especially difficult for me. There was no way of knowing what was to come; what this season would look like. I was treading into uncharted territory.

After completing the long process of checking my things in and getting everything moved into my room, the staff called us all into the dining room for a going-away party for the interns. At one point, they asked me to stand up and introduce myself. To my pleasant surprise, people immediately came up to introduce themselves and talk to me. Everyone seemed so nice. I felt welcomed here, not only by the staff, but the girls as well. They received me with open arms and I noticed my defenses began to melt away. It seemed we all shared a special bond—we were there to get help, work through our issues, and gain freedom in the debilitating areas of our lives.

☙ ❧

Lisa

The new girls had to wait two weeks before they could make or receive calls. I knew the policy was designed to give them time to concentrate on getting into new habits. During that time, they would be enveloped and saturated with scripture and love, and they would be getting their minds focused on what they needed to be working on. But those two weeks seemed to drag on *forever*.

The girls could receive calls on Saturdays, with each caller limited to one ten-minute call. Then on Sundays, the girls were allowed to make two ten-minute calls. That was it. Not much time for catching up and not nearly enough for a mother and father who hungered to know how their daughter was doing, to hear all the details about her new life, her pregnancy, etc. Fortunately there were two of us, so Gene and I placed our ten-minute calls to Jaime back to back, giving us more time, and she usually made us one of her calls on Sundays.

During our first call, even with so little time allotted, I immediately noticed something different. I detected a certain softness about Jaime that had never been present before—an undeniable gentleness in her manner and in her speech. Was such a change possible in so short a time? Yes, apparently so! Two weeks of praise and worship with classes teaching the Word and how to live a godly life had already begun to produce recognizable fruit.

A couple of weeks later, we applied for Jaime's first weekend pass. Mercy allows each girl one every six weeks if they're progressing well, and she was granted one for September 20. We were excited about our visit. Not only did we miss her terribly, we felt it was important to be there as often as we could to support her and spend time with her. We were also looking forward to having Brian, her older brother who lived nearby, come join us.

We couldn't wait. The six weeks that had passed since we walked through those doors leaving Jaime at Mercy Ministries had been a *long* six weeks. We treasured the precious phone conversations with her, but now we would get to be with her and catch up.

Amid making the arrangements for our first visit, I found myself wondering again about how we were going to pay for all of this. What about the birthfather? Will he help out in any way? Once the worry began, I had a hard time getting my thoughts about it to stop.

I finally mentioned it to Gene. He thought about it for a few minutes and then simply told me not to worry about it; God would take care of it. "And actually," He said, "It might be better if the birthfather doesn't help. If he has no financial part in any of this, Jaime may have more freedom in the decisions. I believe she is being led by the Lord every step of the way and I want her to be as free as possible to make the decisions for herself and the baby."

I immediately felt peace. Thankful to be able to put my emotions to rest, I gave the whole thing to the Lord and told Him I would trust Him with it.

❧ ❦

Jaime

The week before my parents' visit, I finished my "Decision Making" class with the other "pregos," the endearing term the other Mercy girls called us. After weeks of class, talking and praying about both parenting and adoption—even making a field trip to a baby superstore nearby to get a realistic idea of the cost of parenting—we each made a short presentation to the group about our decision and handed in a list of reasons that led us to it.

Mercy required this list to be written. If the mother had a difficult time later and wanted to change her decision—which sometimes happens once the mother gives birth—the staff could show it to her and ask what had changed. Usually, the reasons hadn't changed and seeing the list would empower the mother to move forward with her previous decision.

When I arrived at Mercy, I had already been thinking and praying about this decision for months and had a deep sense about where God was leading me. Although I went to the classes and kept an open mind about it all, when it came time for the final decision, I still felt peaceful about placing my baby for adoption. I had a sense this was not my child to parent.

So the presentation made it official. I told the group and my counselor the decision was to place my baby with a loving family.

A few days later Mom and Dad flew in for my first weekend pass. I could hardly wait to see them. Although I had already made several good friends at Mercy, I missed my family so much. They picked me up Friday afternoon and we headed to the hotel where Brian met us for the weekend. Trying to have quality time while living out of a hotel room made for an interesting adventure, but it didn't matter; we enjoyed simply spending the time together.

Those 48 hours were over in the blink of an eye and before I knew it I was back at Mercy. Little did I know the Lord had a surprise in store for Mom and me. The ultrasound appointment to find out the baby's gender was scheduled for Wednesday, but Mom was flying back to Colorado Tuesday, missing the appointment by one day. I really wanted her there, so I asked the Lord to move it up to Monday The hospital was known to be very strict with their appointment scheduling and the likelihood they would change my appointment was slim. Pushing worry, fear and doubt aside, I stood in faith, asking the Lord to answer my prayer…and he did! I called early Monday morning and they had just had a cancellation and could fit me in that afternoon.

It was so special having her there for the ultrasound. I can't imagine how anticlimactic it would have felt not having her with me to share the moment.

The big moment finally arrived…and I'm sure you can imagine my excitement when I found out I was having a boy! Mom and I were thrilled. And I knew it would help me bond with him better. Instead of saying "my baby just moved" or "it just moved," I could refer to "him." And it felt good. It was as if a missing piece to the puzzle had just been found. Talking to him and praying for him became much easier and now I could dream of his little face.

※ ※

Chapter 11

God Kisses

⁂

Jaime

The next day, I had my weekly session with Janet, the Director of Adoptions at Mercy. My next step was to make a list of the characteristics I wanted in the adoptive parents. The adoption department would take it and look through their profiles of approved couples for the ones that best fit my description.

I didn't realize until the time came to make the list that the Lord had been forming it in my heart for weeks. When I sat down to write it out, it surprised me that I didn't have to put much thought into it. Compiling the attributes and characteristics seemed so easy.

This was the list I handed to Janet that day:
- Both to be born again, non-denominational Christians.
- Married at least five years.
- This, their first marriage.
- This, their first child, but with the desire to have more.
- Not able to conceive. *(I wanted this to be a true gift for the couple.)*
- The man to be 6' or taller. *(I am 5'11" and the birthfather was 6'.)*
- Both to have blond to medium brown hair. *(Mine is medium brown.)*
- One or both to have blue eyes. *(Mine are blue.)*
- One or both to be musical. *(I come from a very musical family.)*

- The wife to be a stay-at-home mom. *(I didn't want my child to be raised in day care.)*
- To live in the south.
- To have a dog or want one.
- To love to travel.
- To be 28 and 32 years old. *(I had always felt their ages would be 28 and 32 and that's what I wrote on the official state document, but just before handing it in, I changed the ages to 27 and 31.)*

☙ ❧

The next morning, September 25, my counselor came to my room and knocked on the door. She held a black photo album which she handed to me. In that short time they had already found a profile of a couple who met *every one* of the desires on my list.

Their names were Dan and Kari and:
- They were born again, non-denominational Christians.
- They were about to celebrate their fifth year anniversary.
- This was their first marriage.
- This would be their first child, but they wanted more.
- They were not able to conceive naturally.
- He was 6' 4" tall!
- She was a beautiful brunette and he was a handsome, dark blond.
- They both had blue eyes.
- They were both musical and he was an established drummer.
- She was an artist and worked as an interior decorator but planned to stay at home.
- They lived in the south.
- They had two dogs.
- They clearly loved to travel.
- And…at the time, she was 27 and he was 31. *(However, they would both have birthdays in the next two months, so by the time my son arrived, their ages would be 28 and 32!)*

I couldn't believe it. How amazing of the Lord to grant my *every desire*. My adoption counselor told me they would bring other profiles that met my criteria; that this was only the first. However, as

I opened the book and looked at a portrait of them, my heart leapt and I *knew* this was the couple who would raise my son. I just knew. They looked so in love and were obviously a fun-loving people. It was so like the Lord, too —they looked strikingly similar to me and the birthfather.

As I looked through their profile, it impressed me to see what care and attention to detail they had put into it. I thumbed through each page, smiling at the pictures of them, their family and friends, and their travels to Europe and abroad. It felt like I had known this couple for years; as if I were looking at a photo album of good friends, not of complete strangers.

Then I read the note towards the back, written to the birthmothers considering them as potential parents. Kari wrote, "Birthparents that have the strength to give their children better opportunities through adoption have my utmost respect. I think it is the single most selfless act in the universe." This resonated within me in a deep and profound way.

Although I thought they were most likely the ones God had chosen to parent my son, I decided to look at a few others, just to make sure. This wasn't a decision to make hastily. At the end of my next counseling session with Janet, she handed me three more profiles.

Journal Entry:
I knew from the first page or so of each profile they weren't the ones. Within 30 minutes I handed her back the profiles and told her I had chosen Dan and Kari! She was thrilled. Ever since I told her what I wanted in a family, Dan and Kari had stuck out in her mind. I had such peace and joy about them and knew without a doubt they were the ones God had chosen from the beginning of time for this baby.

After getting special permission, I called Mom to tell her the news and she freaked out. She couldn't believe I had already chosen a family. She said she got chills from hearing the news. I couldn't get a hold of Dad so I called him tonight and told him the news with Mom listening in. It happened so quickly. I thought it would take me weeks to find and choose the adoptive parents. I don't even think it has hit me yet! Wow.

Lisa

Jaime's list astonished me. It was so long, and so very specific. When I mentioned this to her, she simply stated, "Mother, God already knows the couple He's planned to be the parents of my child. It's my job to listen to Him and to get the specifics so he ends up with the right ones!"

Wow. She was right. God knew. He had already chosen them and had prepared this for them as well as for us. With so many people wanting to adopt, the best way for Jaime to get her baby to this particular couple was for God to tell her all the things to put on her list.

Seeing how Jaime had progressed to such a place of incredible faith in just a matter of a few weeks touched me deeply. She expected great things of the Lord and apparently this kind of thinking had become normal for her now. I felt very much like Mary, the mother of Jesus, as I treasured all these things in my heart.

To hear how the Lord so perfectly answered every requirement for the adoptive couple created an explosion in our faith. She told us the couple wanted to meet her, and a date had been set for lunch the following Tuesday, October 8 (another new beginning). She was excited and nervous. She hoped they would like each other and that they would get along. She told us she and Kari looked so much alike, they could be mistaken for sisters, something very important to Jaime. She wanted the absolute best for her baby and knew that if he looked a lot like his parents, it would be one more thing that would help him as he grew up.

We could hardly wait that next week-and-a-half to hear about her lunch with Dan and Kari. Saturday dragged on and on as we waited for the time to call her. I continually reminded myself to calm down, to remember Saturday was her only day to sleep late and catch up on her personal "to do" list. Also, the other girls had phone calls they were taking, as well.

When we finally had her on the phone, she bubbled with excitement. They hit it off immediately. She said Dan and Kari were as excited as she was and they talked and laughed like they had known each other for years. Energetic and fun, they were exactly the kind of people she wanted her son's parents to be. They came with a list of questions, curious about her background, hobbies and interests, and about the birthfather.

Kari showed Jaime sketches of the nursery she and Dan planned to paint and decorate in a zoo theme for the baby and showed her the paint swatches. She described the murals she had designed for the walls to make it look as if his room were right in the middle of a zoo. They asked her what she thought about it, and, of course, she was delighted. Her son would love growing up there!

ᘛ ᘚ

Jaime

Meeting Dan and Kari for the first time went much better than I could have dreamed. I think we were all a bit nervous at first, but it didn't take long for us to warm up to each other. After talking with them a little while, I told them what had happened the night of the gender ultrasound.

"After that amazing, yet exhausting day, I couldn't wait for my head to hit my pillow. Lying in my bed, I thought about the events of the day. *I'm having a boy!* My heart smiled. I was so delighted. I seemed to drift off quickly, but right in that place between awake and asleep I heard the Lord whisper,

'His name means Gift of God, Mighty Warrior.'

I remember thinking, *Wow… Thank you, Lord!,* and I drifted off to sleep. The next morning my roommate, Heather, and I got up and looked through the entire baby name book for names that mean "Gift of God." After writing them all out, I found myself drawn to the name Brennan. I loved the sound of it. That was it! His name would be Brennan. I began secretly praying the adoptive couple would want to keep it as a part of his full name."

After telling them the story, I asked Dan and Kari if they would consider keeping the name, Brennan, for at least his middle name. They both smiled and nudged each other and Kari let out a little laugh. God had told them the same thing; his name was to mean "Gift of God." *How incredible is that?*

The Lord didn't give either of us a specific name, but the meaning instead—and it matched perfectly. They had chosen the name, Nathaniel, which also means "Gift of God" for his middle name. It amazed us to see how God confirmed this to all of us.

Then I asked if they had chosen a first name, and I will never forget their response. They glanced at each other with a cute smile, as if they were wondering how I would respond to what they were about to say. Just the night before they looked through the name book, and this one name jumped out at them. It doesn't run in their family and it wasn't a common name but they liked it a lot:

Maxwell

I couldn't believe it! There was no way they could have known. Maxwell is my grandfather's, my father's and my brother's middle name. The first boys in the last several generations in my family have this name, and now, my son would carry on the tradition.

We just sat there for a moment in complete astonishment—completely in awe of God. How much more confirmation did any of us need to know that my son was meant, all along, to be raised by this precious couple? God had ordained this from the beginning of time, and we just witnessed this beautifully intricate plan of His come alive firsthand.

So, his name would be Brennan Maxwell until the adoption ceremony. Then it would legally change to Maxwell Brennan Nathaniel.

Lisa

Jaime's story left Gene and me speechless. The Lord had done it again. I'm sure He danced around with as much delight as we did. For a few seconds we just stared at each other in complete silence.

Everything began to take on a supernatural feeling. I marveled at God, at the plans He had for Jaime and now, obviously for her baby, Brennan Maxwell. And I was amazed at what He was accomplishing in and through Mercy Ministries.

That evening we called Brian to tell him the news. We knew he would be excited to hear about the lunch meeting with Dan and Kari and how fabulously they all got along, and especially about the amazing story of the baby's names. He, too, absolutely loves God, trusts Him and enjoys seeing Him work in our lives. And he holds a special love for his little sister, so, he got a kick out of hearing that God had told her the name of the baby and she had picked out "Brennan."

He also loved the fact that Dan and Kari had heard from God about the names of the baby, but when he heard the name they had come up with was "Maxwell," he let out a yell, and then simply added,

"Well, you know what it means don't you? ...
... Maxwell means Mighty Warrior!"

Chapter 12

Dreaming with God

Lisa

As the preparations for Jaime and Brennan were progressing, life continued to be very full for me. We lived on a ranch outside Steamboat Springs and there was always so much to do in addition to my full schedule of private piano and voice students.

I started my days with the Lord and had a stack of books at the edge of the sofa in the family room. Ready for me to dive into each morning were my Bible, a couple of books I was reading, and my journal. Having journaled for years, the Lord had impressed me to get organized, keeping everything in one place. I bought a three-ring binder and put my favorite scripture and a picture of the beautiful scene out our front window on the front cover. Then I added dividers for sections that would keep my prayer request list, prophetic words, notes on books, etc., separate from the journal itself.

I enjoyed keeping the prayer requests separate like that because I could run my eye down the list every day, my heart simply agreeing with each one. Since they came out of my prayer time, I had already prayed for them before adding them to the list. Occasionally a few jumped out at me and I would pray for them again.

At some point in the early fall during my morning time with the Lord, it dawned on me that with Jaime in her last month of pregnancy during December, she wouldn't be allowed to fly home for Christmas.

Mercy gave the girls two weeks to spend the holiday with their families, but she wouldn't be able to do that. We would have to have our Christmas together as a family in Nashville. As I began thinking about how that would look, it occurred to me I should begin *dreaming* about what I wanted, and then list each detail as a prayer request in my journal.

As you can see from Jaime's list, dreaming was not new to our family. God had been teaching us about it for years. It comes from Psalms 37:4, "Delight yourself in the Lord, and He will give you the desires of your heart."[12] It literally means we're to love and enjoy Him as we soak in His love for us. He then plants His desires into our hearts, causing us to want them. Delighted, we talk to the Lord about them, asking Him for them, which in turn delights Him. Then He gives them to us and they manifest in our lives, delighting us all over again, creating a wonderful cycle.

Early on, we learned that our first step was to pay attention; to learn to recognize what was in our hearts. What *were* those desires? Once we knew, we could move ahead into that cycle and promise. It's amazing how much it stirs up hope and excitement and it's fun watching to see what God does.

The most recent and spectacular example for us was the ranch where we currently lived. Gene casually asked us one night after dinner to dream about what we would like in a house. The kids and I were familiar with his dreaming, so we went along with him. He had been talking off and on about wanting a place that was closer to our horses. We had moved them several years ago to a pasture right behind our subdivision, but until that night, I didn't know he wanted them even closer.

He began to tell us how he would love to have the horses even closer. It was difficult going somewhere else to feed and water them every evening, especially on a snowy winter night. And when they managed to get through the fence it was exasperating to have to drive to the field where we kept them, find and catch them and bring them back. He said he would love to have a house with some acreage away from town a bit. Not too far, though. He wanted the corral right out the back door with a small building nearby to store the hay and all their gear and tack.

Jaime jumped into the conversation with great enthusiasm and said she wanted a pond on the land close to the house.

Brian wanted a large area right by the house for snowmobiling.

I wanted to have trees. Then, later, after some further dreaming with Gene, I added that I would like to have a log house, but with drywall interior walls (I didn't want a rustic look). I wanted it to be about four years old, not brand-new, but old enough to have window treatments, most of the bugs worked out, and, of course, the yard should already be landscaped.

Sure enough, not too many months later, we found ourselves living that dream!

- Gene got his house out in the country with some acreage.
- The corral stood out the back door behind the tree-lined backyard fence, so you couldn't see the corral, but it was just footsteps away.
- A small outbuilding was located near the coral; perfect for storing gear and tack.
- There was plenty of room for us to store our hay.
- Jaime got her pond! It was just in front of the house and off to the side. A beautiful view from the large front windows.
- Brian's snowmobiling area was a huge ridge just to the west of the house—acres upon acres; perfect for snowmobiling (and horseback riding, walking, cross country skiing, snowshoeing, etc.). The area also included several ranches to the west where we were given permission to be on their land .
- And I got my house:
  - Exactly 4 years old
  - Log exterior
  - Drywall interior.
  - Small, but well-built and beautiful!!
  - Trees, not as many as I'd envisioned, but a few special ones were included. One out front that looked like a Celtic cross and one on the far side of the pond with huge branches that created the perfect quiet place to have coffee or lunch or to pray.

Having experienced answers like that to our dreams in the past made dreaming for our family Christmas in Nashville relatively simple. As wonderful as things had been turning out, lately, it had still been a stressful time for all of us. I wanted and needed this Christmas to be special. But what did I want it to look like? It would be the first time in almost a year all four of us could gather for more than a couple of days.

A thought dropped into my mind—to dream really big, ridiculously big—then see what God would do with it. He had already done so many incredible things with Jaime, the adoptive couple, and the baby's name, etc. I wondered what He would do with Christmas in Nashville.

To start with, I knew I did not want us living out of a hotel room. Four people in a hotel room for two weeks, anytime, would be both difficult and expensive. We certainly wouldn't enjoy visiting and celebrating Christmas like that. There had to be a better way.

So, what would I like? I decided to shoot for the stars. I would love to:

> *Stay in a home,…*
> *a big home…*
> *how about a beautiful home?*

Then my dream began to expand. I thought about finding a rental home, but again, that would be expensive. Ideally, I would like to:

Exchange houses for the Christmas holidays with someone in Nashville.

People did it all the time. It might be a possibility. It would mean a lot of work getting our house ready and securing our private things, but it could be done, and would cost considerably less than renting a home for two weeks. That went down on my list. A few days later I added:

Beautifully decorated for Christmas. And the next day or so, I added,

With a housekeeper.

Wow! My dream for this vacation kept growing! A thought flitted through my mind to call a couple of friends in Nashville and ask if they happened to know anyone who might be interested. The first call proved to be nonproductive, but as I started to call the other couple, the Andersons, I felt a definite hesitation in my heart. No, this wasn't the time. So, I wrote their names down on my list and decided to try later.

Every day, as I scanned the list and saw their names, I paused to see if I should call that day. *No, not yet. Too early in the fall.* I was content to wait. Christmas was still a few months away.

Finally, on our next weekend visit with Jaime, while finishing lunch at Brian's house, I sensed a gentle nudge to call the Andersons. I explained the situation, that we needed to spend Christmas in Nashville, and asked if they knew anyone who might be interested in swapping houses for the holidays. Susan told me they didn't know anyone, but that they needed a caretaker for their home while they were away for Christmas, and asked if we would consider doing it!

Oh my gosh! They have a huge, lovely home in Nashville! As we talked further, she mentioned…

"The housekeeper comes once a week."

Chapter 13

Back to Nashville

Lisa

Shortly afterward, Gene and I began looking forward to Jaime's next weekend pass. She was eligible for one in late October and we wanted to fly there to be with her. Mercy's policy required that parents present their request no more than two weeks in advance and it always took several days to hear back about the approval. That put us inside the 14-day advance window for good airfares and I was getting nervous. I thought, *Didn't Mercy realize the extra expense of flying when you had less than a two-week notice?* Of course, I knew they had good reasons for their policy, but it was frustrating, nonetheless.

During a phone call with Jaime, the subject came up and I thought we might talk about it for a few minutes. She simply replied, "Just trust the Lord with it, Mother. He knows what you need and He'll work it out."

That was all! Then she went right on to the next thing. Wow—another wonderful surprise. Gene and I had lived our lives like that as much as we could, trusting God for things, and yet, here *she* was encouraging *me* in a moment of anxiety! I loved it. (Plus, I noticed her gaining a respect for simply following the rules…with no complaining.)

This newfound sweetness and gentleness continued to emerge more and more in Jaime's demeanor. This, along with her increased ability to trust God with everything in her life, astounded us. She was changing right before our eyes. I had asked God for this for such a long time, for years in fact, and here in the midst of this strenuous trial I was witnessing the fruit of my prayers. God was using this difficult situation to bring about incredible changes in her, accomplishing in weeks what might have taken years.

As it turned out, I couldn't make flights work for us for that weekend, so I called Mercy to request changing Jaime's pass to the following weekend. After several days of waiting and practicing staying calm about the tickets, they approved our request and I found even better and less expensive flights. The tickets were so reasonable that we could fly all the way to Nashville from Steamboat instead of having to drive the usual three-and-a-half hours to Denver to catch our flight. Just one more lesson in simply trusting God to "perfect those things that concern us."[13]

To be prepared, I brought a book to read called "Dear Birthmother: Thank You for Our Baby" by Kathleen Silber,[14] recommended to me by Janet, Mercy's Director of Adoptions. I hoped to finish it by the time we landed in Nashville. Neither Gene nor I knew much about adoptions, but we wanted to support Jaime the best we could.

The author was excellent at explaining what the birthmother would experience emotionally, legally (I hadn't even thought about that!), and financially, etc. It discussed the different kinds of adoptions, ranging from completely closed (which most were, until recently) to completely open, or anywhere in between, depending on the arrangement between the birthmother and the adoptive couple.

In a closed adoption, the birthmother relinquishes the right to know anything about the adoptive couple, to ever seek her child out or to see him again unless the child seeks her out later in life. They are not allowed to know anything about each other. All records stay closed. This practice, prevalent for many years, was often preferred by adoptive couples because it gave them the most security. However, it was terrible for the birthmother. Imagine carrying your baby for nine months, then turning him over to someone you know nothing about, knowing you'll probably never see or know anything about him again.

I'd also never really considered the feelings of the adoptive couple, how it must feel to desperately desire to have a baby, a family, and to live with the disappointment month after month. Or, after having to have endured expensive and embarrassing procedures, only to have nothing work. This book made me realize what an incredible gift the birthmother presented to this couple; the gift of a life. That stopped me cold. I just had to sit and ponder that for a long time.

I cried buckets of tears on those flights that evening, getting off to change planes with red, swollen eyes and soaked tissues. Poor Gene. He gave up trying to quiet my crying. I'm certain it embarrassed him to sit beside me as I made my way through the book. But for the first time, I got an inside glimpse of what a brave thing my daughter was doing, and what she would have to endure to follow through with God's direction for her. To carry a baby, to feel it move within you, to care for yourself and him, to go through labor and delivery and then hold him...and then place him into the hands and lives of someone else—*that* takes courage. Heroic courage. Her baby would become someone else's baby and someone else's family. She would never be the mother...only the birthmother.

I closed the book and sat for a long time sobbing and praying. It shook me to the core.

The book also addressed the grandparents. *Oh, my goodness, that meant us. What about us? We wouldn't be the grandparents...only the birth-grandparents. And, how in the world did one of those act? How would Dan and Kari want us to interact? Would they want it at all?*

As the plane taxied into the gate at the Nashville airport and the doors opened, I finished the last page of the book. I filled Gene in on as much as I could and we felt like we had a much better understanding of the situation facing our family. This definitely was not just a "Jaime thing," but a family thing!

This trip was going to be a whirlwind. There were so many things planned: a meeting with Cissy, Jaime's counselor to find out how things were going; a meeting with Janet to hear about the adoption and how it all had to be walked out; and a meeting with Dan and Kari for the first time, not to mention all the little things Jaime needed to take care of while being out for the weekend. And we wanted to have time to just hang out as a family and enjoy each other.

While picking Jaime up at Mercy, Gene and I got to visit with her roommate and a few of the other girls we had met during our last trip. I noticed an obvious change in every single one of the new girls. Just like Jaime, a softness had blossomed in them and they talked about the Lord with great enthusiasm. This place, Mercy Ministries, proved that change could happen.

Here, sequestered away from the world in a little spiritual incubator and saturated in unconditional love, these girls continually heard from many people and sources, the message of God's incredible grace, love, and faith. They learned how to hear the Holy Spirit and walk in His gifts and power. They discovered how to deal with issues and problems and release them to the Lord in whom they could find real peace and freedom. This training could benefit every one of us.

I was so thankful the Lord had led Jaime here, and frankly, I found myself wishing for a similar place for adults. Everyone has issues. I wondered how many people are even aware of their issues, much less how to deal with them successfully and get healed from them.

I knew that on the other side of all of this, we would have a new daughter. Jaime would never be the same.

Saturday night brought the event our entire family had been looking forward to. We jumped into the car and headed off to a restaurant in Nashville to meet Dan and Kari. I think we felt a bit nervous, wondering how it would turn out. As the hostess led us to the booth where they were already sitting, I saw Kari, a beautiful dark haired young woman with a calm, sweet look on her face sitting next to Dan, a tall, energetic blond man with a big smile and twinkling eyes. My nervousness melted away as Jaime introduced us and we began talking.

They started by telling us about themselves, their story, and how incredible this whole experience had been for them—the timing and everything. Like us, they stood in awe of the Lord, marveling at how He was working out every detail. They told us how courageous they thought Jaime was and how much her selflessness meant to them. They so desperately wanted a child and were ecstatic about all that was transpiring.

We had a wonderful time and immediately fell into comfortable conversation. Like Jaime, we felt like we had known this gracious couple for years. Kari had brought her paint chips and drawings of the room and she told us about her plans for "Max's room." I loved the way she and Dan kept including Jaime in as many plans as possible. Their awareness of and sensitivity to her feelings made me thankful for their maturity and love for her.

I think it surprised us all to hear him referred to as Max, because we had been calling the baby Brennan. Before his adoption, we'd refer to him in that way, but afterwards, he would be called Max, something we would have to get accustomed to.

We laughed and shared stories about ourselves. Brian and Dan discovered that they had already met each other not too long ago in a recording session. What a small world!

By the end of the evening, we found ourselves looking forward to the coming weeks and months, thankful for all God was doing, and amazed once again at His hand in all of this. God's leading of not only Jaime, but also Dan and Kari, one step at a time was truly supernatural.

The next month found Jaime in a whirlwind of activity and each time we talked to her she had more and more to tell us. Besides her everyday Mercy duties, she stayed busy putting into place all the legalities adoption required. Dan and Kari had agreed to a semi-open adoption, meaning Jaime could correspond with them through Mercy Ministries, and when Brennan turned eighteen he could then request and obtain information on his birthparents.

The next thing on her plate was getting a parental release from the birthfather. Without that, there would be no adoption. He had left for Australia before Jaime discovered she was pregnant. She had contacted him earlier in the summer to tell him about the pregnancy and her plans, and he had been supportive. Then Gene and I had the opportunity to talk to him for a few minutes and extend forgiveness, which had been important to us.

With his release for Brennan to be adopted, things would be well under way.

Chapter 14

Caught Off Guard

☙ ❧

Thursday, December 5

Jaime

Although I didn't have symptoms of a cold or flu, I noticed something just felt "off" in my body over the last several days. I didn't feel like my energetic self and I was growing weak. This was not the common tiredness a woman feels in her eighth month of pregnancy. This was different. With my weekly checkup scheduled for that day, I didn't concern myself with worrying about anything until I saw my midwife.

Rebecca, the nurse on staff at Mercy, drove me to the midwives' clinic. I walked inside, checked in at the front desk and took a seat in the waiting room until the nurse called my name. It felt like every other routine visit.

A number of midwives worked at the clinic and I saw a different one almost every time I went in. This unnerved me, as I seemed more at ease with certain ones, but would not be allowed to choose who would be with me during labor and delivery. I would get whoever was on call the day Brennan decided to arrive.

I was delighted to see one of the more calm and gentle midwives walk into my exam room that day, but as she began to talk, I realized something was wrong. She explained my protein levels were high as well as my blood pressure, both symptoms of a condition called preeclampsia. I didn't understand what this meant or what it was. I had never heard of it before. She explained it was a serious hypertensive disorder that affects both the mother and baby and can be fatal to one or both of them if action is not taken quickly. It occurs in five to ten percent of pregnancies and can be cured only by performing a C-section or inducing labor.

She put me on bed rest until the following day, instructing me to come back to the clinic then and have my levels checked again. At that point, they would decide if this were a false alarm. If not, they would continue monitoring me periodically and I would need to stay on bed rest until the baby's birth.

The moment I walked through the doors of Mercy I was told to get right into bed. *But what about dinner? And class tonight?*

Brooke, my dear friend, got permission to come into my room and bring me dinner since I couldn't go to the kitchen to get it. I could do my counseling assignments, listen to music, read or whatever else I opted to do as long as I stayed in bed.

I felt so lonely that evening. At 7 p.m., I heard the faint whisper of a Joyce Meyer video coming from the classroom down the hallway. I knew everyone was there…that is, everyone except me. Hopefully this would last just one night. But if not, I knew God would give me the grace to get through whatever was to come. Secretly though, I prayed that I wouldn't have preeclampsia.

After what seemed like an hour had passed, I looked at the clock: 7:12 p.m. Time crept by so slowly. I picked up my prayer journal and began to write and then listen for the Lord's reply, as a guest speaker had taught us to do.

Journal Entry:

Ugh, Lord. What a day. I've been feeling bad lately and then today I went to see the midwife and she tells me I have symptoms of preeclampsia. So now I'm on strict bed rest until tomorrow when I go to see her again. Father, I'm just trusting you that I don't have it. I'm not worrying about it—I have total faith in you that everything will be fine and that Brennan will still come on the perfect date you have set for his arrival. I know everything will be fine. You knew this was going to happen since the beginning of time. Please give me more peace about it all and grace to get through this.

Daddy, I love you so much. I want to be your "Daddy's girl" forever. I love how your big arms always catch me when I start to fall. How I feel so protected knowing you're always there watching over my every little move, telling me what to do and what not to do.

Sometimes I know I disappoint you and I hate that. I never want to disappoint you. I want you to be proud of me! I want to find favor in your eyes; to be your Daddy's girl. I never want to come to the point where I can't run into your arms for comfort and love and peace on a bad day. I love feeling your embrace. Please hold me close. I love You, Daddy. Always and forever.

Do you have anything to say to me? I'm listening…

"My little girl, I do love you so much. I'm so proud of you and all you've done. You are so special to me and that's why I love blessing you so much! I'm going to take care of this situation (preeclampsia) so you don't have to worry or be scared. It's all in my timing because <u>my</u> timing is perfect. I'm never going to abandon you. I always have my arms around you, holding you, whether you realize it or not. I'm breathing life into you and restoring what was destroyed. What Satan meant for harm I surely have and will continue to turn around for good. You are in my safekeeping, My shelter, the place he cannot come; he is not allowed. I'm growing you up my child. I'm growing you up into a beautiful princess and I will <u>not</u> let him take that away. He cannot harm you; my hand is on you, My child. You <u>are</u> special to me. I love you so dearly. And yes, you are "Daddy's lil' girl" —My little girl. Don't ever forget that. I love you sweetie, my sweet child."

His words touched me so deeply. I didn't know how, but I had a profound "knowing" He was going to take care of everything and I would be fine. The next day's appointment would provide more answers on the days and weeks to come. It couldn't come quickly enough, so I laid my head down and drifted off to sleep.

Friday, December 6

When I woke up the next morning, I quickly brushed my teeth, washed my face and got back in bed. My appointment was at 1 p.m., so I had a little time to work on reading assignments and get some good rest. I had become very tired these days. The amount of energy needed to take a shower seemed equivalent to running a marathon.

Once again, Rebecca took me to my appointment where they checked my weight, protein levels and blood pressure. Then Carole, another of the midwives, walked into the exam room to speak with me.

Carole was a woman of great stature, fairly tall with brown hair and prominent features—an attractive woman who reminded me a great deal of my aunt. She was also strong and forthright; steady as a rock. Truth be told, Carole intimidated me very much and scared me a bit with her slight abrasiveness.

Now, although I have a strong will, I will be the first to say I turn into a sissy when it comes to physical checkups. I get nervous in the appointments and whimper like a child when my blood is drawn. Carole, I'm sure, noticed my anxiety and probably figured I should have been more accustomed to these by now, being eight months along. Not so. My wimpy-ness in this area would continue.

My due date was January 3 so I was still four weeks early. To make matters worse, my protein levels had continued to rise since yesterday and my blood pressure was still high. Carole told me I needed to stay on bed rest, specifically on my left side, until Brennan came. If the levels dropped, we would wait until he came naturally. However, if they stayed high, they would have to induce me early. She didn't know how early but made the point that if they waited too long our lives would be at risk. They scheduled me to return on Monday and would possibly induce labor.

I'm sorry, what did you say? Induce me? This early?!

Although it wasn't the first time I had heard this, it was most certainly the first time it sank in. I was in shock. Surely this wasn't happening to me.

On the way back to Mercy, I felt numb. My lips didn't know how to form words so I just sat there quietly in the car as Rebecca drove. An abundance of questions and feelings flooded my mind and soul. *I can't have Brennan this early. I thought I had another four weeks. I'm not ready... I'm not prepared for this....*

Eventually, I managed to calm my thoughts and emotions. Then I felt it. Somewhere within me I felt a deep sense of peace. So deep that if I hadn't quieted myself, I never would have known it was there. Somehow the Lord was in this; somehow He would take care of me. He said He would never leave me nor forsake me. If I ever were to believe this promise, now was the time. I had to trust Him. I could not do this without Him, and even if I were capable of doing it alone in my own strength, I didn't want to. I knew He had Brennan's and my best interest in mind.

The moment I returned to Mercy I called my mother. I missed her and wanted so badly for her to be with me, now more than ever. She needed to come to Nashville, and quickly.

☙ ❧

Lisa

That afternoon, I was busy teaching the last few lessons for my music studio's Christmas piano and voice recital, scheduled for Sunday afternoon. I always enjoy these final preparations; encouraging each student, fixing a spot here or there, and having them practice everything they'll be doing as their part of the recital. It's important to polish each part of their performance so they feel as comfortable as possible at the recital. Even so, with parents and friends in attendance and all the other musicians and their guests, emotions always run high.

In the middle of all of this, the phone rang. When I'm teaching, I typically don't answer the phone, but I had told my family in the event of an emergency, if they needed to reach me, to hang up and call back immediately and I'd know to answer it. When the phone rang a second time, I excused myself and told my student to continue through the piece and I'd be right back. I sensed it was Jaime, and sure enough, I was right.

She told me she had just seen her midwife who placed her on strict bed rest for preeclampsia, a condition that could possibly put both her and Brennan in danger. She was told to take it very seriously and to lie on her left side until Monday when they would recheck her. If there was too much protein in her urine, they would have to induce labor. Obviously scared, she asked if I could come right away.

I comforted her, prayed for her, and told her I'd arrange to get there immediately. I knew she was in a safe place, surrounded by loving women who would take good care of her.

After I hung up, I exhaled slowly, told the Lord, "Okay…Here we go!," and put my trust in Him for every detail, knowing He had already made all the arrangements necessary and that everything about to unfold was in His hands. A deep peace enveloped me. In the natural it made no sense, since I knew I had lots of pieces to wrap up even before I could catch a plane. But I felt that "peace that passes all understanding"[15] that scripture promises us.

Saturated in this peace, I calmly went back to teaching my lessons, able to give each student my full attention. Fortunately, one of the mothers there that afternoon loved to help with our recitals. I told her that due to a family emergency, I had to leave the next day for Nashville, but saw no reason why we couldn't go ahead and have the recital as planned. All the students were well prepared and could go right on without me. She told me not to worry; she would take care of everything.

When Gene came home for dinner, I filled him in and we discussed our options and made plans for my trip to Nashville. A few preparations still needed to be done for Sunday's recital since I wouldn't be there; including recording accompaniment tapes for all the vocalists and printing out the programs. Gene offered to take over as emcee and assured me it would be fine. He would explain the situation and tell everyone how I would have loved to have been there. He would tell my students how proud I was of their progress and how much I loved them and their families. I could rest assured they'd have a wonderful recital and I'd be free to deal with whatever came up with Jaime.

Thankful for such a loving and able husband, I turned my attention to the trip. I needed to find a flight, purchase tickets, and pack for… goodness, how long I didn't know, but I imagined I might end up staying through Christmas. Gene would remain behind until the time came for him to be there.

We felt the best thing to do was to check her out of Mercy and find an extended stay hotel nearby. There, I could be with her and take care of her, either until Brennan was born or we moved into the Anderson's home for Christmas, whichever came first. Being there by herself on bed rest, stuck laying on her left side while the girls were in classes would be difficult. I didn't want her to have so much time on her hands that she would become sad and lonely. And truthfully, I was looking forward to having some time alone with her during this special time.

It amazed me how easily things came together, not that it didn't take a while. I finally got to bed around 2 a.m., tired, but knowing it would all be okay. Since I didn't fly out until late that afternoon, I'd have time to finish wrapping up the recital and get everything into Gene's hands.

Saturday, December 7

Lisa

I had been noticing the numbers again, encouraged by God's prophetic message through them. That day, the 7th, spoke to me about the *completion* and *perfection* of all the things God had been doing in this season; Jaime's (and my) growth and all the preparation for Brennan's birth. I was literally wrapping up things here so I could leave and step into our "new beginnings" the next day, the 8th.

I also noticed that when flying, even my assigned seats and the gate numbers had been prophetic these last several months. God seemed to enjoy encouraging us in this way.

༄༅

Jaime

After the first day of strict bed rest, which seemed to last an eternity, I found myself starting the second, with no specific end in sight. Questions began to stir in my mind: *How long would I be here? A couple of days? A few weeks?* I was torn. Though I dreaded the thought of being in bed on my left side for a few weeks, it meant I could still be with Brennan, feeling him kick and move within me. A strong bond had formed between my baby and me, as I hope happens with all mothers and their unborn children. I had never seen his face or felt him in my arms, but he was very much a part of me and I *knew* him and cherished every moment I had with him.

Regardless of how long I still had with Brennan, I felt this season starting to come to an end. The wheels on this crazy ride on which I was about to embark had begun to turn, and I had no paradigm for the spins and loops coming my way.

The Lord had been so faithful to continue giving me grace and peace through it all. I noticed, however, that if I began thinking too much about the coming days and weeks—how delivery would be, how hard it would be to let Brennan go—I found myself in a place of fear and unrest. God extended grace to me every day. It became my daily bread. He gave me what I needed for each moment. If my thoughts traveled beyond that, too much fear would grip me. I knew I had grace for that day and when the next day came, He would be faithful to give me grace for it, as well. One day at a time. His mercies are new *every* morning.

Thankfully it was Saturday, which meant the rest of the girls at Mercy had free time. I had made great friends over the months and they all came to my room, periodically, to check on me. I felt so loved!

Early in the afternoon I heard shuffling in the hallway. I got quiet to see if I could hear what was happening when a few of my dear friends appeared in the doorway with a large TV. They had asked permission to bring it into my room to watch movies. How sweet! The hours did seem to go by slowly, so this would help keep me entertained. They set it up where I could see it while lying on my left side. Their thoughtfulness and care meant so much, as well as the fact the Mercy staff allowed it. I had never heard of such a thing. However, that is not the only special thing they allowed me during my bed rest.

∽ ∾

Lisa

"No one is allowed in the rooms. Even *Jesus* would have a hard time getting through the door!," the young woman at the front desk at Mercy Ministries exclaimed to Brian. Perhaps it was the "points" he'd made with the girls and staff bringing donuts from time to time on Saturday mornings, or Perhaps it was the genuine love he had for his sister. But Brian got special, and I mean *special* permission to bring Jaime dinner and visit her in her room that night.

"Mom, you don't get it," Brian exclaimed. "The *girls* can't even go into to each other's rooms without permission. And guys are *never* allowed to go in there. The fact that they gave me permission to bring her dinner and visit with her was amazing. I was walking in incredible favor."

Concerned about Jaime being isolated and lonely and wanting to do something about it, he had called me earlier to get the recipe for

"No-Peepin' Chicken," a family favorite, and had been excited about preparing it for her. All the girls had gone to a Christian conference, so he and Jaime found themselves alone in the home with the exception of one staff member, making it calm and quiet.

Jaime asked him if he wanted to feel her tummy, but feeling odd and hesitant about it, he said no. Later, she said, "He's kicking; do you want to feel him? Here, put your hand in mine," and in what he described as, "a motherly and gentle way," she took his hand and placed it on her tummy. A few seconds later he felt Brennan kick.

Before he left, they prayed together and, the way he told it, it seemed as important to him as it was to her. This was a family ordeal, and he was an integral part of it. The tone in his voice, as he related this story, told me a special moment had occurred.

Chapter 15

The Waiting Game

◈ ◈

Sunday, December 8

Lisa

When I arrived Sunday afternoon at Mercy to pick Jaime up, everything was quiet and serene and the peace of God permeated the air. The staff all moved and spoke in relaxed, soft tones and went about their duties soundlessly. They appeared to be secure and grounded spiritually; excellent role models for the girls who came to live there. What an amazing place; so different from the world outside.

Heather,[16] Jaime's roommate and good friend, came to meet me and escorted me to her room. Moving at barely a snail's pace, Jaime hadn't finished packing when I arrived. That gave me time to visit with her and a few of the other girls who either popped their heads in the room or lingered in the hallway.

While waiting, I met a few of them and got an even deeper insight into Mercy Ministries. Christine, one of Jaime's close friends, a calm and confident young woman, impressed me as solid and mature in the Lord, especially for her age. She told me she'd been there 11 months and occasionally thought it was time to be released, but each time God had more for her.

I also met Stephanie, their bathroom mate, a girl with the saddest eyes I'd ever seen. She was a wisp of a girl, extremely thin, frail and withdrawn. She weighed only 85 pounds. I was told later she had just lost a dear friend who died of anorexia while waiting to get into Mercy.

Brooke, a beautiful young woman with genuine Southern gentleness, came in and out, helping Jaime with her things. Jaime told me later that Mercy allowed her to choose two girls to be with her during her entire hospital stay, rotating their shifts and Brooke was one of them; Christine was the other.

A young woman named Amber came in the room bubbling with excitement, looking for Jaime. She had attended a conference the night before and had asked God for a few free videos or a book, since she couldn't afford them. Not only had she been given a book, but also a check for $100 as well. And, the second night of the conference, someone gave her a free video. She wanted Jaime to know because she had reached out to her with such kindness and had been praying with her. It was Amber's first experience of God answering her prayers like that.

This kind of faith was common at Mercy Ministries. The people there took God at His Word, and expected and experienced the power of the Holy Spirit operating in their lives daily. I loved it. This is what I consider to be the *normal* Christian life.

Because the girls had no scheduled classes on Sundays, Jaime's room was flooded with friends who loved her and wanted to check up on her. It was wonderful, but it certainly prolonged the packing process. Jaime's slow, tentative movements, foggy thinking, and delayed responses made me feel as if we were in a slow-motion film. It took forever. Plus, everything, absolutely every item she planned to take had to be documented. Thank goodness for Heather, who knew where things were and helped, because Jaime had to stay in bed as much as possible.

When we finally finished packing we went downstairs, only to go through it all again to get her officially checked out. At last, tired and hungry, we were in the car and on our way!

As we entered our hotel room sometime later, Jaime and I both noticed the room number, 555 (grace, grace, grace), and smiled, recognizing the prophetic significance. *Thank you, Lord. I'm so glad you're in this with us. We need you!*

Monday, December 9

Jaime

The next morning we received a phone call from Janet, the adoptions counselor. Kari had called her wanting to talk to me to see how I was doing. However, Janet needed my permission before Kari could be given my phone number. *Of course it was fine.* Within a few minutes we received another phone call and I answered it.

"Hi! This is Kari… … …," and she used her last name. I was stunned. Until that moment I didn't know her last name, and was not supposed to!

She asked how I was doing and if there were anything she could do for me. She wanted to get together, but, of course, since I was on bed rest, she wondered if she could come and either bring Christmas cookies or a movie to watch. *How thoughtful.* At that point, she offered to give me her phone number. As I wrote it down, I got to the last four digits and the numbers became scribbles.

I hung up the phone, literally shaking. *What was God doing?* Under a semi-open adoption, we were required to go through Mercy for any type of contact with each other. However, she had just offered her personal information so I could call her directly. *Are we moving toward an open adoption? Oh Lord, that would be wonderful.*

Although in the fall I had wanted a semi-open adoption, my heart had been gradually changing. The more I grew to know Dan and Kari and the closer I got to Brennan's due date, I realized I truly desired an open adoption. I wanted Brennan to know me growing up and to have memories of me at an early age. For him to know that it was out of the great love I had for him that I placed him for adoption, and for him to experience that love first-hand.

Everything was coming together, with God truly orchestrating it all.

Lisa

Later that afternoon I drove Jaime to the midwife clinic for her 2 p.m. checkup. After examining her, Carole sent us right over to the hospital for the doctor to check her and get a decision on the preeclampsia. As they ushered us into a delivery room, I couldn't help but notice the room number—#5. *Yes, Lord, thank you for your great grace, love and mercy.* I was immediately thankful for that little sign that spoke volumes to me about the Holy Spirit's presence there to do, in His power, whatever needed to be done.[17] I felt myself relax a bit as we walked into a beautiful, softly lit room.

Jaime

Although Mom seemed relaxed, I was freaking out inside. *What is going on?!* We were in the hospital, in a labor and delivery room. *I am not ready for this! Lord, what are you doing?! This does not feel right. I know we are in Room #5, and you always speak to me through '5's, but this doesn't seem like your timing! I'm scared, Lord. I need you so badly right now.*

The doctors and nurses came in and out of the room, checking on me and taking my blood pressure while we waited for an answer. *Was it time to induce?* I had been there quite a while before they released me and told me to come back in two days for another check as I was not ready yet. My protein levels were okay, but I still needed to stay on strict bed rest until I came back in.

It was becoming evident I would eventually have to be induced. Coming in every couple of days to be checked was a good indication I would not carry this baby full term. Although relieved to leave the hospital that afternoon, I knew the day would soon come when they would tell me it was time.

Lisa

As we left the hospital, Jaime seemed weaker than ever and didn't have much to say. The air felt thick as I wearily drove us to Brian's house where we were going to join him for dinner. Jaime would be able to rest there while I checked out extended stay hotels on the internet. She could possibly be on bed rest for a month and since we still had two weeks to go before we could move into the Andersons' home, I needed to find a place with a kitchenette where we could fix our own meals and stretch out a little bit.

After a little searching, I found a place I thought would work well and we went to take a look at it. It was roomy and nice and within easy driving distance of the hospital, so I reserved a room starting the next day.

As we returned to the hotel, I realized how overwhelmed I felt. Gene usually takes care of all of this; moving and loading luggage, securing rental cars, choosing hotels, and making the financial decisions. I knew how expensive it was for us to make these trips back and forth to Nashville, and now, the possibility of staying in a hotel for a couple of weeks made me anxious again. I called to update him earlier and talked with him about the upcoming expenses, but he reassured me everything would be okay, to go ahead and find something that would work for us and not worry about the finances. The Lord would work it all out.

Tuesday, December 10

Tuesday, I packed us back up and moved us from the hotel over to the Candlewood Suites, our new little home away from home. It felt good to be going to a place where we could relax more, even though we'd have to wait one more day before we really settled in. No one-bedroom units were available until the following day, but after that, we could unwind and enjoy each other until Brennan was born.

The room number, #353 (miracles and grace), made me smile and I mentioned it to Jaime as we walked in. It was comforting, as well as a bit comical, that the Lord would continue to reassure and encourage us in this way.

Wanting to fix a good dinner for Jaime, I made a quick trip to the grocery store and picked up some food and Christmas lights to perk up the room a bit. Since we were going to be here a while, it seemed like a good idea to make it festive. We had a good time together while I prepared dinner, chatting about nothing in particular, just enjoying being mother and daughter. Later Jaime worked on her crochet project, a baby blanket for Brennan, while I read. Nothing too exciting; just a relaxing evening.

Chapter 16

It Begins

Wednesday, December 11

Lisa

Wednesday morning I repacked and moved us *again* (*Ugh!*) to the other room; the one bedroom. This was our last stop before moving to the Andersons' home for Christmas. Thank heavens. I looked forward to settling in and not having to move again for a while.

We couldn't help but notice the new room number, #108—"8". Any time now, those "new beginnings" would begin.

As I started unpacking Jaime's things, I had the sense I didn't need to. I noticed it a second time a few minutes later, but continued anyway, reasoning that I'd feel more settled and I could certainly use being settled, right?

As it turned out, I should have paid attention.

That afternoon Jaime and I went back to the midwife clinic for her appointment where they did a quick exam and told her she needed to be checked by the hospital staff. Deep in thought, we slowly walked the short distance from the clinic to the hospital. Once again, we found our way to Labor and Delivery, where a nurse led us through the swinging doors and down the hallway to the delivery rooms. As we passed room #5, our previous room, I wondered what room number the Lord would give us this time. As we entered, we both noticed the plaque next to the door—#8. We gave each other a knowing look, and wondered if this were "it."

This room resembled room #5 from our Monday visit, softly lit with subdued, comfortable colors. A chair stood in the corner that folded out into a bed and a tall cabinet beside the bed opened up disclosing the medical equipment. What a wonderful place to have a baby. So different from the cold, sterile room where I had my children, under what felt like a floodlight. I was thankful for this place and for the kind nurses attending to Jaime. As we waited for them to return, we sat on the edge of the bed, deep in thought.

෴

Jaime

Jill, the midwife on call, came in and helped hook me up to the monitors. She took my vitals and ran several tests. While we waited for the results, she explained what could happen as she thought the tests would show they would need to induce labor. Her soft voice and sweet demeanor put me at ease.

Often preeclampsia causes the mother to have seizures, so they would give me Magnesium Sulfate, which would make me feel horrible and extremely thirsty, but would slow my reactions and body responses to prevent them during delivery. It would take several hours for it to take effect and then they would induce labor.

Is this "it," Lord? Is this your timing—for Brennan to be three weeks early? Mom and I both wondered. With all these things weighing on our minds, we listened carefully to hear what the Lord was saying, to see how He was leading us, and to get confirmation about it.

෴

Lisa

Okay, Lord, what shall we do here? Are we to induce her labor? We called Gene to update him and told him we'd call back as soon as we knew the test results. After the call, he closed the door and paced back and forth praying. It was a scary time for him, and it seemed like forever, waiting for the phone to ring. He hated feeling so helpless. As the head of the family, accustomed to leading, making decisions and taking care of things, not being there with us made it difficult for him. Knowing Brian was there to act on his behalf helped him accept the situation.

☙ ❧

Jaime

It took quite a while for the nurse to return with the test results. She told us right now Brennan and I were both fine, but my health and strength were quickly deteriorating. Then she said,

"Let's deliver you before things get worse."

Those words rang in my ears over and over. For a moment, my brain felt like mush. The room was spinning and I could not focus or come to grips with the fact that this was "it."

Wow. Everything was happening so fast. *How could it be that I'm here at this point already?* It seemed like only a month had passed since I found out I was pregnant, and a week ago that I arrived at Mercy. Brennan and I only had a little time together and it hadn't been near enough.

☙ ❧

Lisa

That phrase again! "Let's deliver you," or "Let's get her delivered." We heard it several times over those next few hours and each time it hit me in the strangest way. Perhaps I'd always thought of delivery as the baby being delivered, not the mother. For example, a deliveryman delivers his package. *He's not delivered of the package*...although, it is true. I simply had never thought of it that way. It made me wonder if God planned to use this whole situation in a much broader way than I could imagine or understand.

The nurse urged Jaime to agree to inducing labor and told us she'd give us a few minutes to discuss it. We called Gene back to give him the news and get him in on the decision. He said he had sensed God's peace about it, as had we, so we agreed. We told each other, *"Tomorrow we are going to have a baby! Tomorrow, 12/12, will be Brennan's birthday!"* We called Brian and told him the news and invited him to come join us.

Jaime and I began to get excited. Yes, this was it. Sometime the next day we would meet Brennan. We'd get to hold and cuddle him.

It was strange, not having Gene there with us, and probably a lot more difficult for each one of us than I realized. He had always been with us during important or critical events, however, with everything happening so quickly, there wasn't enough time for him to join us. No flights were available, and driving was out of the question. The trip, on a good day with dry roads, took twenty-three hours. Driving over the high mountain passes through the Colorado Rockies during the winter, possibly in severe weather, would make the trip even longer. No, he couldn't possibly make it in time.

Terribly disappointed, we realized he couldn't be with us for Brennan's birth, so we finally decided to have Gene wait. We agreed to keep one ear listening to the Lord, in case he should come earlier, but we kept our original plan of having him come for Jaime's Christmas break so we could celebrate Christmas as a family and attend the adoption ceremony together. As much as we hated this decision, it seemed to be the best one.

As we waited for the nurses to get everything ready, one of them realized Jaime hadn't eaten anything since that morning and it was already after dinnertime. She told us once they began to give her the Magnesium Sulfate she wouldn't be allowed to eat again until after delivery. Even though she wasn't supposed to, if we kept it a secret, she would bring her a cup of soup. Jaime thanked her and quickly agreed. It was perfect timing, because shortly after the nurse brought her the soup, they announced they were ready to start the Magnesium Sulfate.

I cherished the time we spent together there in that room. We talked quietly, marveling at all that had occurred; all the Lord continued to do and show us. Every so often, we'd just sit quietly, not saying a word, pondering all that had happened and wondering about all that would transpire over the next few hours.

Suddenly, she gasped and turned to me and said, "Mother, I've been here before!"

                    ✤

Jaime

As I sat there on the end of the bed in the delivery room, my legs dangling over the edge, I happened to glance up and notice the quilt on the wall opposite me and the round clock to the left of it. Then my eyes landed on the cup of soup on the table to the right of me and a nurse walked in and said "Jaime, we're almost ready to start your IV." It was strangely familiar. Somehow I felt I had been here before. I remembered this like I had lived it already. *But how?* Immediately, the Lord reminded me of a short but vivid dream from a few months before.

In August, I dreamt I was pregnant and my baby came early. Although the reason was unclear, I had a strong sense we were both fine and healthy. Sitting on the end of the bed in the delivery room, my legs dangling over the edge, I looked up at the wall opposite me and noticed a quilt hanging on it with a round clock just to the left. Next, I glanced down at a cup of soup on the table to the right of the bed and immediately a nurse walked through the door and said to me, "Jaime, we're almost ready to start your IV."

After waking up, the only thing I remembered was that my baby came early and we were both fine. But that day, the nurse's words triggered the memory of the rest of the dream.

Amazed and excited, I told Mom about the dream, pointing out every detail. "God *was* speaking to me through that dream! He knew Brennan would be born early and was telling me *everything would be fine!*"

I felt a rush of peace come over me. The Lord had known all along this would happen and I'd wonder what to do. This was His timing, his good and perfect timing!

                    ✤

Lisa

After a while, we heard a knock on the door, and Brian poked his head in the room with a big grin. It surprised him to walk into a room that looked more like a hotel room than a hospital room. He looked a little disoriented for a few seconds, but then came right up and hugged me. Then he turned to Jaime and said, *"Hey, J, how's it goin'?"* and hugged her and said something funny. That's how the rest of the evening went.

We loved having him there as he livened things up considerably. Normally, when things get heavy, Brian provides the comic relief and he kept things light for us all that evening. He and Jaime joked and talked together for quite a while. He teased her about the popsicle she was allowed to suck on, and posed with her for a few pictures.

We relished our time together, each of us understanding the preciousness of the moment, the gravity of the situation, and sharing the anticipation of Brennan's birth sometime the next day—all creating a special memory and bond between us.

༄༅

Jaime

Before this whole experience, my brother and I shared what I would call a normal sibling relationship. We fought for our parents' attention, knew each other's "hot buttons" and got pleasure out of pushing them often. But we loved each other very much and had fun together when we were not arguing. However, as our family walked through this difficult time, a new, sweet, tender side to our relationship began to develop. These months that I had been pregnant drew us together in incredible ways. It was the start of the loving relationship that developed into the closeness we share today.

Unfortunately, the Magnesium Sulfate running through my veins not only made me sluggish, but affected my memory. Although I can remember scenes from the days at the hospital, they consist more of moments than actual blocks of time.

One of those moments I hold dear took place between my brother and me that night in the Labor and Delivery room. The nurse put a Pulse Oximeter on the tip of my index finger that registered my heartbeat and the oxygen levels in my blood. Its little red light glowed there at the end of my finger. A little while later, Brian walked into the room, came over to my bed and hugged me. We exchanged a few words and then he noticed my glowing red fingertip. As if acting out a script, we both brought up our hands and touched the tips of our fingers together and said simultaneously, *"ET, phone hooome."* It still makes me chuckle to this day. Our sense of humor is very similar and we have a great time together. I needed to laugh. Everything had been so serious and dramatic and our laughter changed that.

❧ ☙

Lisa

As the evening progressed, Jaime became increasingly lethargic; a bit funny, actually, as her response to everything slowed down and she…mooooved…and…taaaalked…reeeea…lly…sloooow…ly. Finally, we prayed together and said good night. Brian left and I spent the night on the little pull-out bed in the corner. Off and on nurses came in to check the machines and her blood pressure, waiting for the right time to induce. I hoped we could get some sleep because the next day was going to be a big day for all of us.

❧ ☙

Chapter 17

Brennan's Birth

Thursday, December 12

Lisa

Early the next morning, the nurse told us they could start inducing labor at 7 a.m. and we would probably have a baby by early afternoon.

Sure enough, at 7 a.m. the nurses came in to get everything ready. A while later, the midwife came in to check on Jaime and fill us in on what to expect. It surprised both of us to see Carole, the no-nonsense one, walk through the door. Much to our disappointment she, not Jill, was on call that day and would be delivering Jaime.

I had really come to appreciate Jill's soft and gentle manner and wondered how Jaime would fare with Carole. However, as it turned out, I found myself thanking the Lord several times throughout the day that she had been in charge. Carole's straightforward approach ended up being exactly what Jaime needed.

By this time, the Magnesium Sulfate was in full effect, so even though she was in the early stages of labor, Jaime was not very responsive or talkative. The morning seemed to drag on forever and I called Gene and Brian occasionally to update them, but for the most part I spent the time just waiting.

Carole came in from time to time to check Jaime's progress and finally announced, "Okay, it's time to deliver her."

Jaime

When it came time to push, all I knew to do was what I had seen in the movies or on TV–push with *all my might*, so that's what I did. Half an hour later, Carole told me the moment had come but I was pushing too hard, so I needed to pull back and push *gently*. However, I was too much in the moment and only let up a little.

Minutes later, at 1:52 p.m. on Thursday, December 12, my precious son entered the world! The nurse wrapped him in a blanket and softly laid him on me. At 5 lbs. 11oz., Brennan was so small, but a perfect and beautiful baby. For months I had felt him move and had grown to love him more with every kick. But in this moment when I first met him—first laid eyes on him—I realized the immense love I had for him. I had never felt a love like this before—the love of a mother for her child. I couldn't believe how close I'd come to aborting this life. I would never have known this love and wouldn't have had the privilege of bringing this beautiful child into the world. How close I came to not having him in my life. The Lord preserved him and kept him, and I was grateful for that. I knew I would do anything for him, even if it meant great pain on my behalf.

Lisa

Now, I'm sure you'll consider me prejudiced, but this tiny little child had none of the newborn wrinkles or oddly shaped head that many babies do. He was perfectly beautiful. After Jaime held Brennan for a while, the nurse took him over to the side of the room to weigh and check him. When she finished, Jaime offered to let me hold him.

Cradling him gently in my arms, I soaked in every bit of those few moments with him. I gazed at his tiny fingers and eyelashes, his darling little lips and ears and the angelic look on his face. I already loved him deeply.

Oh, Lord! How wonderful to hold this precious little bundle. He is so perfect. Thank you for him. Thank you for sparing his life and keeping him safe through everything. Bless him, Lord, and protect him.

I searched his little face to see who he looked like. Surprised, I discovered my eyes looking back at me, and yes, that was my nose and mouth! *Oh, my goodness, he looks like me!*

Being in Nashville with Jaime during this crucial time was a blessing for me. I wanted to be able to love and support her, to pray, and to do what I could to help. I wouldn't have had it any other way, but honestly, it was one of the most difficult things I had ever done up until that point. Jaime should have experienced this with her loving husband by her side; not me, her mother. The two of them, knowing they would soon be holding their baby—a child they would take home to care for and love; to play with and help him grow. I should have been out in the waiting room with Gene and perhaps Brian, looking forward to being grandparents and an uncle, waiting anxiously to hold our little one for the first time and know we had years and years together.

But, it was not to be. My heart ached for her, aware that instead there would be only a few hours to hold and love and cuddle her baby, her own flesh and blood, before she would give him to another. I grieved for her, for Gene and Brian, for myself…and for Brennan, too. Would he understand that Jaime did this all out of her intense love for him?

It occurred to me that perhaps I should feel sad, knowing my little grandson would not grow up with us and that we'd never have a grandparent-grandchild relationship. However, with all the other emotions and circumstances, I simply didn't have time to explore those feelings. I needed to be "in the moment" for Jaime. I knew the Lord would work all those things out later, so I pushed them from my mind and focused on what was happening in the room. Sensing Jaime yearning to have Brennan back, I walked over to the bed, kissed his tiny head and placed him gently back into her arms.

Watching Jaime with Brennan was precious. She couldn't take her eyes off her son. Tenderness and love radiated from her as she talked to him, gently caressing his tiny head, nose and little fingers. Clearly, she had loved this child a long time. They must have had long conversations during her pregnancy, and now they could finally talk face to face. His little eyes were on her constantly as he cuddled there peacefully in her arms.

They spent a long time together, as it took an inordinate amount of time for Carole to finish up. Long after I laid Brennan back in her arms, Carole was still at work. She quietly indicated she was having a problem getting the bleeding to stop, so I lifted the whole thing up to the Lord. That last hard push resulted in considerable injury. However, Jaime didn't even notice. She lay wrapped up in her own little world with her son.

Chapter 18

Gift of God

Jaime

Before too long, I asked for the phone so I could call Dad. I missed him so much. I knew he ached as much as I that he was so far away and couldn't be a part of all of this. I wondered why the Lord planned it this way, without him being here. Just hearing his voice made everything right.

After hanging up the phone with Dad, I called Dan and Kari and invited them to the hospital to see Brennan. I knew the immeasurable love I felt for him represented only half of the parental equation. They had tried for many years to have a child of their own and I couldn't imagine the heartache they experienced. I wanted them to have the privilege of holding their baby as a newborn since they may never have the opportunity again. I didn't know if it would be hard for adoptive parents to bond with a baby who wasn't their own and I wanted Brennan to feel as much love as possible. I hoped this would help them all feel that bond, beginning the very day he was born.

Shortly after my phone calls Brian came in to see me and to meet Brennan. It was so good to have him there with us, especially since Dad couldn't be there. He made my heart smile by just walking in the room. The first thing he did was come over to the bed, hold my hand for a moment, and ask how I was holding up. Then his eyes moved toward Brennan resting in my arms and I could tell he was mesmerized. How could one not be by this beautiful, little one.

He handed me a present; an adorable stuffed animal puppy with a red bandana around its neck. It brought me such joy. *Thank you, my sweet brother.*

When Dan and Kari arrived, Brennan was in the nursery and I was resting. They came to see how I was doing and we spent time together talking. Their genuine concern for my well-being touched me deeply. I knew they were excited about Brennan, to know their son had just been born, so it meant a lot that they cared about me, as well.

Lisa

I couldn't believe my ears when Jaime said she wanted to call Dan and Kari to come. She hadn't even had time to enjoy her baby, to relax, or to sleep. She had just given birth and was worn out. As I walked across the room to get the phone, I found myself marveling at her and her heart for them. I guess it shouldn't have surprised me; after all, they would be Brennan's parents. I had witnessed the raw determination in Jaime from that day when she first heard his heartbeat, and knew she would do the best she could for him. Her love for him was so great. All she could think about was him, so for her to make them as much a part of his birth day as possible was completely like her.

When they arrived, I hugged them as if they were family. Well, they *were* family now. We visited for a while and when Jaime asked if I'd go get him from the nursery, they came with me. We spent several minutes outside the nursery window gazing at him. They were so excited…and I was excited for them! After years of waiting, God had now fulfilled their dream of having a baby.

We rolled the bassinet back to Jaime's room together, talking about all God had done to bring things to this point—the timing of their decision to adopt, the timing of their acceptance as prospective adoptive parents by Mercy Ministries, the way God had told them Brennan's names, and so many other things—all miraculous. Between enjoying all of this and finally getting to see Brennan, we were all soaring.

Back in the room, Jaime held Brennan for a few minutes and then asked Kari if she would like to hold him. I'll never forget the sweet look on her face as she reached out her arms for him and drew him close. She tenderly looked over the one who would soon be her own.

As a matter of fact, tremendous love, grace and godly maturity emanated from Kari and Dan in general. The gentle way they treated Jaime blessed me deeply.

After Dan and Kari left, Brian and I stayed with Jaime and Brennan for the rest of the day. Brian's tenderness toward his sister touched me deeply. I loved having him there and enjoyed witnessing the special time he had with his little nephew.

He admitted it scared him to hold Brennan at first. He didn't know how to hold him or what to do with him. "It was surreal, a pinch-yourself moment," he said. He remembered thinking, *Holy Cow, I'm an uncle now!*, as if it hadn't occurred to him until that very minute.

He looked at the clock to check the time, then looked down at Brennan, lying in his lap, facing him. He played with his little fingers and studied every little detail, every cuticle and tiny fingernail, the little wrinkle in his fingers, his big blue eyes, and so on. When he looked back at the clock, it surprised him to see that almost an hour had passed. He had been completely mesmerized by Brennan. He had no idea how it had happened. For him, time had simply stopped.

The entire experience of Jaime's pregnancy affected him profoundly. Being only 23, he hadn't realized the challenges girls face and the kinds of things they have on their minds. For instance, before meeting any of the girls at Mercy, an eating disorder was just subject matter for a TV show. But, being around girls who were facing it as a life or death situation made him have to stop and think. Furthermore, he hadn't given much of a thought about his stand on abortion until he had to face it through Jaime's situation.

He had always thought pregnancy was the mother's choice, but now he found himself questioning it all. It astounded him to know how many people want to adopt and that more than two times that amount of babies are aborted.

With all these thoughts whirling in his mind, he was suddenly brought back to the present and looked down at this beautiful little child. Jaime could have chosen to not have him. But what a gift he was.

Jaime

Later that evening I found myself marveling in God's love for me. How incredible. He had given me so many confirmations about Dan and Kari being the parents for Brennan, the meaning of his name, and even about the dream I had in August, confirming to me that it was His plan for me to be induced and Brennan be born three weeks early.

But that's just it. He wasn't born early, nor a minute late. 1:52 p.m. was the perfect moment. Pieces started coming together as I began to realize just how many "8"s (new beginnings) surrounded Brennan's birth and this whole experience:

- He was born at 1:52; the numbers add up to 8;
- On December 12, exactly 8 months to the day after his conception;
- In Labor & Delivery Room #8;
- Eighteen weeks, to the day, after I arrived at Mercy on August 8;
- The same date (August 8), Dan and Kari were accepted as an adoptive couple for Mercy;
- I met Dan and Kari for the first time on October 8.

How divinely intricate God's plan was. Everything happened in perfect sync. I was in awe. He really cares about *every single, seemingly trivial* detail in our lives. And for Him to give me the dream in August, remind me of it, then bring it to pass as a way of comforting me and telling me we were walking in His will...*Lord, you are so good!*

As I pondered all the amazing pieces to this puzzle, the Lord revealed one more thing to me. He brought to mind the first two nights in May, after I had the ultrasound and heard Brennan's heartbeat for the first time. I had awakened at specific times in the night and it was so unusual, I wrote them down in my journal. The first night I woke up at 3 a.m. and 4:44 a.m.; and the next night at 3:33 a.m.. This is what the Lord revealed to me:

- There were a total of four "3"s (3:00 and 3:33), which, when added together equal 12.
- There were a total of three "4"s (4:44), which, when added together equal 12.
- When you put them together, you get 12-12 or December 12—Brennan's birth date.

How incredible! The very day in May when I chose life for my child, the Lord showed me His perfect design in it all. In a way I could not have conjured up myself, He planted a little clue seven months prior to giving birth to show me everything lined up perfectly to His will and timing. He was in this…all of this. And would be with me every step of this journey. Even with the hardest days yet to come when I would have to let Brennan go, I knew the Lord would be right there beside me giving me what I needed for each new moment.

Chapter 19

The Scare

❦ ✧

Friday, December 13

Lisa

The next morning, I woke up early and spent some time reading my Bible and praying. Still worn out from all the hustle and bustle of the last few days, I appreciated a real bed to sleep in and a good night's sleep. What an ordeal this had been. And, it certainly wasn't over yet. We had some tough stuff coming our way for the next few days for which we would really need God's strength to get us through.

As I started to get ready to go to the hospital, Brooke, who had stayed with Jaime the night before, called and said Jaime wanted me to come. There was no rush, but she wanted me there. I inwardly kicked myself for not just getting dressed and going to the hospital as soon as I woke up. I could have read and prayed there all day long. After all, our time at the hospital with Brennan was short enough as it was.

I hurriedly showered and dressed and just as I opened the door to leave, Brooke called again to find out how much longer I'd be. Realizing Jaime really did need me there and there was a reason to rush, I jumped in the car, drove to the hospital and parked, then raced down the stairs and across the street as quickly as my legs would take me.

Once inside the lobby, I nearly ran into a large crowd waiting at the bottom of the elevator. *Well, of course! Isn't this always the case when you're in a hurry?* I quickly surveyed the scene, mentally checking my options, then, being the "patient person" I am, I looked for the nearest stairwell and raced up.

As I passed the nurses' station, one of them called out to me, "Go on in. They're waiting for you." *Waiting for me? Why?*

Pushing the door open, I walked into a "Twilight Zone" moment; surreal and movie-like. The room was dark with only a small flood lamp illuminating Jaime and her bed in a pool of light. It cast a soft glow over the large assembled group of doctors and nurses completely encircling her bed.

As I walked in they all turned, as if on cue, and looked at me, but not a word was spoken. "Hello," I offered, and I walked over to Jaime and gave her a kiss and a little hug, noticing she looked as pale as a ghost. Then I found my place in the circle between her and Brooke. As I looked up at the group, someone introduced me and one of the doctors began to explain the situation. "We need a decision and we need to make it *immediately*. Jaime has lost a great deal of her blood, more than half of it, and we want to give her a transfusion."

Fear gripped me. Outwardly, I could tell I appeared calm and collected, but on the inside I was certainly not. I asked the group if we could have a few minutes together and they agreed, but asked me to keep it brief. Time was of the essence.

❦

Jaime

In my entire life I have never felt as weak as I did lying on the bed that day. The effects of preeclampsia and the significant blood loss had already taken their toll on my body. To say I had no energy is a gross understatement. I felt *lifeless*.

I cannot recall most of the day, only a snippet here and there. It felt like my mind was barely functioning.

When the doctors came in that morning to talk with me they said I had lost more than half of my blood, which explained my ghostly appearance and severe lack of energy. They presented two options. First, I could have a blood transfusion, which they recommended with my condition. The risks included the possibility of having an allergic reaction to the new blood and a chance of infection (Hepatitis B, HIV, etc.), although it's a rare possibility as donors are heavily screened. The second option, not having a transfusion and allowing my existing blood cells to multiply by themselves, would take approximately three months. I'd continue to feel lifeless and lethargic until then.

How could I possibly live like this for three months? There was no way. I did not feel good about waiting and building the blood supply back in my own strength. *In my own strength.* Something about that phrase struck me, but I didn't understand until later. I wanted to see what my parents had to say and in what direction God was leading them, so I patiently waited for my mother to arrive.

Lisa

My mind raced. *Blood transfusion?* I knew Carole had trouble stopping the bleeding after Brennan was born yesterday, but I had no idea Jaime had lost that much blood. I'd heard stories about blood transfusions, people contracting AIDs and all kinds of other diseases from them.

Gene, I need you. We need you. Why aren't you here? You make these decisions so easily. My mind attempted unsuccessfully to pull my thoughts together.

We had both agreed he would come the minute he sensed God leading him to. However, despite everything going on, we had not sensed the Lord telling him to come. So, here I was, walking through it all with him by phone—not in person as I would have preferred.

Jaime and I talked and prayed for a few minutes, and then I called Gene to explain the diagnosis and options, asking him what we should do. He is always able to sense God's peace so well, and I couldn't seem to find it anywhere, so I trusted him to hear from Him.

He asked for a few minutes to pray about it and said he'd call me back. Then he closed the door to his office and paced back and forth, seeking God's answers. Through the many hours he'd spent praying during our hospital stay, Gene had definitely gained strength from the Lord. When he called a few minutes later, he quietly and simply told me to go ahead with the transfusion. He had a great deal of peace about it.

Just that simple. *Thank you, Lord, for this man.* What a blessing to have someone you love and trust hear from the Lord with you when you need help.

Jaime agreed, saying that's what she wanted as well. We called in the nurse and gave our consent.

In those next few minutes, I called Martha, our pastor's wife, a mighty warrior woman of faith and prayer with a strong anointing for healing. God had worked incredible miracles through this woman and nudged me to call her. *Lord, thank you. That's exactly what I need to do.*

I explained the situation and she immediately began to pray into the situation with the power of the Holy Spirit. She bound up a spirit of death over Jaime and prayed, "I see you as you lie there in your blood, and I say to you, "*Live!*"[18] This shall *not* be unto death! You shall not die but *live and proclaim the works of the Lord.*"[19]

Wow. I had been so deep in the trenches, going from one thing to the next, I hadn't even recognized Satan's attempt on Jaime's life. I was stunned, but grateful to have someone from the outside with the ability to discern the enemy's strategies, praying with authority into our situation.

When we hung up, I immediately sensed relief. Strengthened and encouraged, I felt a huge part of the load lift off me.

Thank you, Lord, for your leading, your timing, and putting the perfect people in our lives.

Shortly afterwards, a group of nurses came in and quickly pulled things together to whisk Jaime out of the delivery room and into a private room to start the transfusion. They asked Christine, who had come in to switch with Brooke, and me to step out of the room as Jaime needed several hours to rest.

Jaime

Sometime that evening, before we turned the lights out to go to sleep, Christine came over and sat down on the bed next to me. We both gazed at the IV bag hanging above me, filled with blood, running down the tube into my arm. Someone else's blood. Someone I had never met.

Who was this person? Male or female? Were they in their twenties, thirties, forties? What were they like and what was their story? Gratitude overflowed to the mystery donor. They chose to donate their blood to give others life—to give *me* life! I sat there a moment and then without thinking about what I was saying I uttered, "It's like the blood of the Lamb." Only when the words left my mouth did the Lord open an incredible revelation to me.

The doctors said I had lost more than half my blood, so after the transfusion, this person's blood would account for more blood in my body than my own. The two were becoming one—and would remain that way for the rest of my life. Nothing I could do would ever separate it. *Nothing*. I would *never* be the same person again.

When we give our lives to Christ we allow Him to permeate our very being. He becomes a part of us. But what the Lord was showing me was in that moment, His blood which He shed for us, runs through us and we become more of Him than we are ourselves. *More of Him than of us*. We truly become a new creation.[20] Nothing we do or say will form us back into the person we were before we gave our lives to Him.

And like this new blood now flowing together with my own, when we accept Christ it is impossible to separate us from His love. [21]

The Lord also showed me something about how He moves and works. If I had chosen not to have the blood transfusion, but had decided to build back my physical strength on my own, it would have taken me several months. With the transfusion it would take only a matter of a few days.

When we do things in our own strength; when we choose to rely on ourselves and not on God, things are harder and take longer and are more dangerous and risky. When we do things in His strength and rely on Him—lay down our lives and our plans for His will—things go much, much better for us. He knows what is best for us and our lives and He *wants* that for us.

And we know that in all things God works for the <u>good</u> of those who love him,
who have been called according to his purpose.[22]

Chapter 20

Cherished Moments

Saturday, December 14

Jaime

With the blood transfusion complete, my energy started increasing the following day and the color began returning to my pale complexion. I felt much better, although extremely sore all over. I don't recall the reason, but apparently the nurses never put a "port" in, either to draw blood from for the tests or to give me blood. Instead of having one in place they could quickly draw from, they came and stuck me with a needle *every single time.*

I must have been pricked 20-25 times, or at least that's what it felt like. My arms and the tops of my hands felt mutilated and tears welled up in my eyes when the nurse walked through the door holding the last needle. I was exhausted and just plain tired of hurting.

My last full day with Brennan all I wanted was to hold him as much as possible. If all went as planned, I would be discharged from the hospital the next day and would have to say goodbye to him. But I couldn't think about that as it was all too hard. As long as I held him, it seemed everything was right in the world.

He was so beautiful. His big blue eyes gazed into mine so intently. Sometimes it seemed as if he was talking to me, widening his eyes and moving his lips as if telling me a story. I listened to every word and cherished them in my heart.

Such an incredible bond had already formed and I knew he felt it, too. Somehow even at a couple days old he knew me. He knew I was his mother and felt protected in my arms. He would squirm and fuss but the moment I held him he would get quiet and calm. He was home—a place of love, peace, and rest. Even at my young age, I was this infant's mother; his place of comfort and protection.

☙ ❧

Lisa

God must have kept me in a protective bubble as we walked through all of this, sheltering me from the gravity of the situation. It still hadn't hit me that I could have lost my daughter or my little grandson. That came later. The reality of most of this experience didn't truly occur to me except for the amazing thing Jaime was about to do, give the gift of life, and knowing we were all about to face the most difficult time we had ever experienced.

Despite that, we were continually aware of God's presence and handiwork and it astounded us. And it wasn't just our family, but also the girls from Mercy and even one of the nurses who noticed. Everywhere I turned, something else declared to us—practically yelled out to us—that He was there with us and it would all be okay. We simply needed to keep trusting Him and walking it out. His love was so great, so powerful, and so incredible.

We felt much enclosed in our own little "God world," separate from the outside one. It was bigger than reality to us. We talked constantly about Him and what He was teaching us and showing us. Our amazement and awe for this Heavenly Daddy of ours grew and grew. And, I must say, it was an incredible gift.

No, this was not surreal. This was the only real part—living in God's love and His presence hour after hour after hour. The unreal part was all the things swirling around in the natural world around us like hospital rooms, nurses, doctors, IVs, etc.

Jaime and her friends, Brooke and Christine, had been sequestered in this same little cocoon of God's love, mercy and sweet presence for months at Mercy Ministries. They had soaked in it. They were full of it; saturated with it—with Him. And, guess what? They exuded it. They practically oozed His love, sweetness and gentleness. But, they also "got" it. They understood what this unconditional love would do. They saw it day after day in the lives of the other Mercy girls and in the testimonies of prior graduates who came back to share their victories.

Lord, thank you for the blessing of this time. It has been so precious. You are so precious!

I must have forgotten Jaime had been moved the prior afternoon. When I arrived at the hospital it surprised me to enter the small, rather sterile private room, and not the pretty, soft colored and spacious labor and delivery room I'd grown accustomed to. She was sitting up in the bed with Brennan cuddled in her arms. Everything seemed so peaceful and sweet. The overhead light cast its harsh light on her, so I couldn't tell if she looked better or not. I gave them both a hug and kiss and said good morning. She looked up at me and I felt the sadness that enveloped everything and everyone in the room. This was the last day with her baby. I decided not to dwell on it, but to enjoy the time we did have.

Definitely more alert than yesterday, Jaime came alive after a few minutes. She was excited as she told me about the revelation God had given her about the blood transfusion. I listened to her as she described it all, enthralled at how God had become so real and big inside of her in the last several months.

This had been my heart's desire for Jaime, and now, after years of praying and trusting, I saw that He had used it all—the pregnancy, going to Mercy, the preeclampsia, and even the loss of so much blood—to transform her into this godly young woman, excited about her relationship with Him. *Incredible.*

As she finished telling me about her revelation, she added, "Mother, because of the transfusion, I got to have another day with Brennan!" It was truly "beauty for ashes."[23]

ഏ ൙

Jaime

I knew my time with Brennan was running out. It was almost bedtime, but I couldn't let him go back to the nursery. The nurse asked if I wanted him to sleep with me and I said, "Definitely." They could come back in a few hours if they needed to take him but I wanted as much time with him as possible.

Brennan was already fast asleep as he lay there beside me on the bed with my arm around him, holding him close. I couldn't take my eyes off of him. This miracle, this gift God had given to me—what an incredible blessing. *Gift of God, Mighty Warrior, indeed.*

I lay there thinking about the consequences and what I had succumbed to in making the decision to give him life: the emotionally taxing situations and the physical pain and risk as both of our lives had been in jeopardy. As I looked at him lying there next to me, it *all* seemed *so* worth it. So much so, that I would do it all over again just to have him here. He was worth all the pain and heartache that I had already endured and that which was yet to come.

The love I felt for him was uncontainable. I began sobbing a deep cry. *Would he ever know how much I love him? Would he understand it was out of that love that I chose to do this—to give him a better life than I could give him?*

Tears ran down my face for a long time.

Thank you, Lord, for giving me the strength to choose Brennan's life over mine. You guided my every step and let me hear your voice so I could follow your leading. This path has led us down a road of great blessing. You are such a good and gracious God.

I forced myself to stay awake as long as possible. I knew this was one of the last moments I would have with my son like this. Eventually, exhaustion overcame my determination to stay awake and I drifted off to sleep. At some point a nurse came, woke me, and took Brennan back to the nursery for the remainder of the night.

Although the moment passed, the memory will be in my heart forever.

☙ ❧

Chapter 21

Surrender Day

❧ ☙

Sunday, December 15

Jaime

I woke up and felt sick to my stomach. This was the day I had to say goodbye, so I spent the early part of the morning with Brennan, holding him in my arms as much as possible. I dreaded this day for months. I secretly hoped it would never come; that time would stand still and I could simply remain in the bliss of knowing my child and having him with me.

I thought about something Kari said at a lunch date we had several weeks before. She and Dan wanted me to know they were not pressuring me in any way to place Brennan. If I changed my mind they would understand and wouldn't hold it against me.

What an incredible thing to say. At the time, I started tearing up as I told her I knew it would be the hardest thing I've ever done, but I knew this was God's plan for Brennan's life and ours as well. It was clearly God's will that Brennan be raised in Dan and Kari's home and I was 110 percent positive I would not change my mind about this, no matter how hard it might be.

Holding him close, it was almost impossible not to feel torn between wanting to keep him and choosing the Lord's plan for him. It was evident the Lord had ordained Brennan to be *their* son to raise and parent, and for that to happen, I had to let him go. The decision rested in my hands and I could swing it either way…but it didn't just affect me; it affected my son, whom I adored, and the lives of many others.

So, really, there was no decision to make at all. The way was clear. I just needed the Lord's strength to carry out what I knew was His will for our lives.

> *For I know the plans I have for you," declares the LORD, "plans to prosper you and not to harm you, plans to give you hope and a future.*[24]

His plans are to prosper and not to harm. The Lord does want the best for all of us. His will contains blessings for those who choose it.

Lord, I choose your will, your way. Give me your strength to do this!

Lisa

I woke with the heaviness of the day on me. It had hovered ominously in front of us all for months and had now finally arrived. This morning, Jaime would surrender her child to someone else. The whole situation was heartbreaking. I could only imagine the pain Jaime felt having loved her baby all these months—talking and singing to him during her time alone. She had held him, gazed on him, felt his tiny body next to hers, his little eyes gazing into hers. And they had shared little secrets together as only mothers and newborns do.

Now, because of her, a young couple would have their heart's desire. It was so much like Jesus. She had been so strong, so focused. She continued to walk through it all with great resolve and determination.

Gene and I had witnessed that determination several times during her life and talk about it from time to time. The first glimpse happened on a cold and snowy ski trip when she was five or six. The whole family had warmed up on some lower, easier slopes and had gone to the top of the mountain. We were all only about a quarter of the way down the mountain when it happened. Jaime had already fallen several times. Tired and freezing cold, she "lost it" and said there was no way she could go on. She *quit*!

Well, that's fine, except that it was not the kind of slope where we could carry her or help her down. Though not a black diamond run, it was fairly steep all the way to the bottom. Gene talked to her for a few minutes and told her the only way to get down was for her to ski herself down, and that he knew she could do it. She just needed to be tough and get down that mountain. At the bottom, we could have hot chocolate, something to eat and warm up and rest.

She looked up at her daddy. Then, with great determination and without a word, she turned downhill and skied her little heart out. She didn't slow down or stop until she reached the bottom. I just saw one "S-turn" after another all the way down. When we gathered at the bottom, she was warm, full of confidence, and pretty darn proud of herself.

That same determination rose up the day she heard Brennan's heartbeat for the first time. There was no way for her to quit. She couldn't quit. She *wouldn't* quit. The only way out was through…and she was doing it valiantly.

Thankfully, she had learned good decision-making skills, including looking ahead, planning, preparing, and praying over everything. Then, incorporating the wisdom gleaned through prayer, the scriptures and godly counsel, she walked out each decision.

Of course, that didn't mean any of it was without emotion. This journey had been a continual roller-coaster ride of emotions while she looked to God and trusted Him to bring her through. She was simply continuing to walk it all out. We all were.

But this day, the myriad of feelings would have to wait. We needed to give each moment our full attention.

So, a little before 10 a.m., I drove to the hospital one last time. Frankly, I was tired of that drive. In the last several days, I had made the trip multiple times. I parked in the parking garage, made the long walk over to the hospital, rode the crowded elevator, walked down the hall through the double doors, past the nursing station, and into the room.

Lord, help! I need your grace! I need your presence! We all do. We need you to gather us all up in your arms and walk us through this!

When I arrived, Jaime was sitting in a chair near the window, quietly holding Brennan in her arms. I hugged them and gave them a kiss and we talked until Brian arrived.

Grateful for a few minutes together, I sensed we each needed some "family time" before the others arrived. I asked Brooke, who was there with Jaime, to take a few pictures, knowing we'd want to have some from this last time together with Brennan before he went to foster care. They would help us remember this special day and help Gene feel more a part once he saw them.

Before we knew it, Dan and Kari came in and a few minutes later Janet arrived with Cindy, Brennan's foster mother until the adoption was finalized. It was quite a group. As we gathered in a circle around Jaime and Brennan, we knew we were all here because of this little one. Each one had his own part in this and the Lord had drawn us together for a short time—our lives briefly intertwining.

Fully aware of the importance of this day, I requested we have a time of prayer, not realizing it was on Jaime's "list" as well. Mercy had required that she make a list containing all the things that were important to her during her hospital stay and especially for this last day. This was her life, her child, her decision, and would be her memories. This put her in as much control of the situation as possible.

As I began to pray, thanking Him for being with us through every step, His sweet presence came down over us and filled the room. Like a soft blanket, He wrapped us in His love and a holy hush settled on us; a tangible stillness we basked in for a few minutes.

We prayed for Brennan, thanking God for him, for preserving his life from abortion and through the high-risk labor and delivery, and we prayed blessings over him. God had named him Mighty Warrior, Gift of God, and yes, we believed that was exactly what he was. We prayed God would protect him and he would feel loved and wanted.

After praying for Brennan for quite a while, Dan and Kari prayed for Jaime, thanking Him for her love and selflessness in carrying their "gift." They prayed beautiful prayers of blessing over her. Then we ended up by praying for one another. Something profound had happened here, and we were all very much in awe of our incredible Father.

ൟൟ

Jaime

I was thankful we had this time together before my son left the hospital. The time in prayer provided an appropriate and solid conclusion to our days in the hospital and the right foundation on which to begin the next several weeks between now and the adoption ceremony.

I know many people were praying for me, both in Nashville and back home, and I was grateful for them and felt their prayers daily. But I needed to have people lay hands on me and to *hear* their prayers. The last five days had been the hardest days of my life, both physically and emotionally. Physically, I felt close to death. Emotionally, I reached the highest of highs, giving birth to my child, and the lowest of lows, knowing I was giving him away. I desperately wanted and needed the prayer.

I had thought and prayed about this day about how I wanted it all to go and it turned out even better than I had hoped. After taking a few pictures with Brennan in my arms, it was finally time to say goodbye.

Earlier this morning I had some alone time to process and grieve, so thankfully I didn't break down in front of everyone, although a few stray tears did escape. I stood up, holding Brennan close, then looked down at him sleeping peacefully in my arms; this small, beautiful baby boy. All of this was for him. I kissed his forehead and as courageously as I could, held him out and gently placed him in Kari's arms. At the same time, she and I looked up at each other. She had the warmest smile on her face as she held him. This woman would be an incredible mother. And, she needed to be. I was entrusting her with what I held most dear—my only son.

I had wanted to specifically *place* Brennan in Kari's arms for symbolic reasons. No one was going to *take* my child from me. Even though he would be going to the foster home, I felt a certain order was appropriate as I refused to see my son being placed in the arms of anyone but his new mother. I hated the fact that Brennan had to stay in foster care until the adoption ceremony. If he couldn't be with me, I wanted him to be with Dan and Kari—people who loved him deeply.

I don't ever want him to feel unloved. Although Cindy was sweet, tender and caring, she was not family to him.

Lisa

Jaime stood up, signaling the end of this chapter of our lives. The air was thick with emotion as she tenderly kissed her tiny son's forehead and gently placed him in Kari's arms. Then she reached over and picked up the stuffed dog Brian had given her after Brennan's birth and put it beside him. She wanted him to have something familiar, something that smelled like her, a "part" of her, to comfort him while he was in foster care awaiting adoption into his new family.

Aware that only by God's grace could I be here, witnessing this with such composure and incredible peace, I praised Him for undergirding me—for undergirding all of us with His strength. This moment was the culmination of everything that had transpired over the last few months and the peak of our heartbreak, watching Jaime surrender her child.

I found myself once again thanking the Lord for the wisdom He'd given Mercy Ministries in requiring all these steps be thought through and planned out. She needed to see; no, perhaps we all needed to see Brennan leaving with his new parents, even though it would still be two weeks before he would begin his new life with them.

After they left, Jaime asked for a few minutes alone and I was thankful as I also needed a little time to myself to get alone with the Lord. I needed Him to comfort and strengthen me for the next leg of our journey. Brooke, Brian and I went separate ways to find a quiet place in a hallway. I imagined they had been silently praying for Jaime all morning as I had, but now it was time for us to leave this place and help her move on. I sensed a big part of her left with Brennan when he left the room. She was going to need the Lord in a big way.

After several minutes, we regrouped and went back into Jaime's room, finding her ready and sitting with quiet strength, holding a stuffed dog, identical to the one Brennan left with. She had asked Brian to purchase this additional dog for her and had named it Max, hoping it would help her feel still connected to Brennan. It would be a good reminder of the wonderful few days they had together in the hospital as mother and son. We trusted it would help her to have something to hold close during the hard days of grieving and processing that were surely to come.

❧ ☙

Jaime

When the time came for us to leave, Mom, Brian and Brooke helped me collect my things. I grabbed Max, the dog, and held him close while I sat down in the wheelchair. Riding the elevator down, with all the flowers and cards, I silently reflected on this "Mercy Week." It was hard to believe it had all happened in just five days. Everything had seemed surreal…and now we were all about to step back into time and space. Our lives had been dramatically changed, yet outside the world hadn't noticed, or even paused. It all seemed so odd.

Without warning it hit me like a train. I began weeping the deepest tears I had ever known. There is nothing common or natural about a mother leaving the hospital without her newborn baby. *It felt like my heart was physically being torn in two.* I have never in my *life* felt that kind of anguish. The immense emotional heartache literally inflicted physical pain.

For him to be a part of me, day in and day out for eight months, for us to bond over that time, to give birth to him…and then now not to have him in my arms…I fully believe this to be one of the greatest agonies a person can feel.

Clutching Max the Dog in a headlock with both arms against my stomach, I bent over in my seat and cried uncontrollably. The only thing I felt I had to show for those precious five days was this stuffed animal.

My son, my son, my son! Every part of my being cried out for him. I already missed him dreadfully.

Chapter 22

Life Afterwards

~~

Lisa

I brought Jaime back to the Candlewood with me rather than going right back to Mercy. She needed some down time and we both needed to recuperate emotionally as well as physically. Additionally, I wanted to have some mother-daughter time with her since we had been apart for the last four months.

Despite our still being in the midst of grief and churning emotions, there were several details that needed attention in order to keep the upcoming adoption process moving forward. Setting up temporary insurance for Brennan was the first priority.

I made an appointment for the next day with TennCare, Tennessee's Medicaid program. When the time came for me to leave, I headed off with my instructions. However, once on the loop that circles Nashville, I realized I was missing an important piece in the directions. I didn't know where to get off. I had been told that if I were late, my appointment would be given to the next person in line and I'd have to reschedule. Since we didn't have time for that, it was crucial I not be late. But I had only planned for the amount of time to get there according to the directions they gave me—not enough to include getting lost—so I began to panic.

Lord! Where do I turn? When do I exit this loop? I told Him He needed to guide me because I didn't know where to go, nor did I have a phone number to call. At every exit, I got quiet inside to listen to whether or not this was the exit to take. Each time, I heard nothing. Exit after exit went by and still no urging to turn. Suddenly desperate to get off the loop, I said to Him, *I've got to turn at the next exit! I'll pull into the first gas station or convenience store and get a phone book and call or get directions.*

So, at the next exit ramp I pulled off the freeway, drained, a bit frantic, and quite lost with only four or five minutes to spare. I noticed I was not in a good part of town and the first place to make a call was a run-down convenience store and gas station with some rather sketchy looking people coming and going. I quickly strode in, walking right over to the checkout counter. A large man with a scraggly beard, whom I assumed belonged to the motorcycle parked outside, was talking to the man behind the cash register. When my turn came, I explained that I was lost, almost late for an appointment at TennCare, and asked if I could use the phone book to make a call and get directions.

He leaned over the counter and said, "Now, little lady, pay really close attention, because this is going to be complicated." When I replied, rather tersely, that I really wasn't in the frame of mind for teasing, he turned and walked toward the door. "Come here," he said, as he looked back at me. "I have something to show you," and he walked outside.

Oh, my gosh, now what do I do! I listened to my heart, waiting for something from the Lord, but didn't sense anything at all, other than it would be okay to follow him. So I gingerly followed, telling the Lord I was trusting Him to keep me safe. When the man walked around the corner of the convenience store, I balked. *Lord, are you sure?!* But, again, I sensed nothing. He stopped suddenly and it startled me. But then he turned around, laughed and finally pointed to a tall building a block behind the store and said, "There it is, lady. It's right there. You're not lost, you're almost there."

I couldn't believe my eyes. There it stood, less than a minute away.

Realizing I'd been holding my breath the whole time, I let out a sigh of relief, thanked the man and hurried back to my car. By the time I drove around the corner, parked and found my way inside, I was right on time. *Lord, that was unbelievable. You guided me right to where I needed to be, even though I never really sensed You leading me. It felt more like me just making decisions than You leading.*

The TennCare office was a large and rather sterile government room, noisy and jam-packed with all kinds of people; all of them needing help.

As I stood in line waiting to be called, I thought about the plight of many of these folks and how blessed we were to have had such incredible provision for every need along the way.

I didn't realize, until I was sitting across from the agent in his small cubicle, I had silently prepared myself to be scolded for having a daughter who had gotten pregnant and would need subsidized health care for her child. You can imagine my relief and gratitude when, instead, he treated me with kindness and compassion. And as a bonus, not only was insurance provided for Brennan, but for Jaime as well—a complete surprise.

Returning to the hotel room, I noticed the atmosphere had plummeted from restful to depressing for Jaime. She needed more than just her mother and extra time on her hands even if she did need to rest. She needed to be back at Mercy with all the girls, the activity, love, and support. So, after making arrangements for her to go back, I packed her bag and helped her into the car. The Christmas party, scheduled for that evening, seemed like just the thing to lift her mood and get her going again.

Nothing looked different at Mercy as we parked and walked up to the front doors, but as soon as we stepped in, we were taken completely by surprise. A whole new world greeted us. Astonished, we took in the entire entryway and large living room beyond it. This was no little Christmas party thrown for a few girls at a Christian ministry. True to their vision, the Mercy home was now lavishly decorated for an elegant Christmas dinner party. It was breathtaking.

The girls and staff swarmed to greet Jaime, hugging her and talking excitedly, delighted to have her back. Brooke offered to let her borrow an elegant blouse to help her get into a festive spirit, and led us into the living room to show off the tree and the mountain of gifts under it. Everyone was exhilarated and Christmas party electricity filled the air.

I loved being there experiencing the extravagant outpouring of love Mercy and their supporters showered on these 40 girls, and I was once again deeply touched by their demonstration of unconditional love. Although I was invited to stay–and would have loved celebrating with everyone–I thanked them, wished them a Merry Christmas, hugged Jaime goodbye and slipped out the door.

The next day I picked up Jaime and we headed off to a nearby town for her appointment with the judge to sign her surrender papers. It was quite a drive, but Mercy had chosen this man because of his heart for their ministry and for young women in crisis. We were ushered into his stately law office, lined with custom built-in walnut bookshelves and a massive and handsome matching desk. Sympathetic and kind, he introduced himself and invited us to sit in chairs opposite him. He turned to Jaime and asked if she understood the purpose of the visit. She replied that she did.

Then, in a soft and gentle voice, he began talking to her about her decision to place her baby for adoption and thanked her for her courage and fortitude. "It takes great strength to do this; a thing most people do not…*cannot* do," he explained. Then he leaned forward and, with emphasis said, "I know you are a wonderful mother. I know because one of the characteristics of great parents is their willingness to sacrifice for their children. You are making the ultimate sacrifice of all, and that makes you a wonderful mother."

I was deeply touched. No condemnation. No scolding. No harshness, judgment, or condescension. This man honored Jaime. He understood.

Then, still talking only to her, he told her he also knew that she, too, had a wonderful mother. "Out of all the young women who've ever come through my doors, over all the years I've done adoption work, she is the first mother, ever, to accompany her daughter." Then he turned to me and said, "Thank you for your courage and support of your daughter. You've done an excellent job raising her. Jaime is a strong and brave woman and you should be proud of her."

Wow, I never expected to hear that! All these years I'd been primarily aware of the ways I'd failed her as a mother, yet he just thanked me and told me I'd done an excellent job. He showered me with the same lavish grace he'd poured upon Jaime.

I was acutely aware God was using this man to speak His heart to us. Just like Him, this judge looked beyond the surface and into our hearts and pronounced a sentence of grace and love, of honor and respect over both of us—exactly like God does for all of His children and wants us to do for each other.

He walked both Jaime and me through the legalities of the surrender, reiterating what Janet had explained at our first meeting. Jaime would have ten days in which to change her mind about placing Brennan for adoption. During that time, he would live in foster care, with Mercy Ministries handling everything—visitations with him, communication with Dan and Kari, and the terms of the adoption, whether closed, open, or semi-open. At the end of the ten days, Brennan would be adopted by Dan and Kari.

As we completed the paperwork, the judge smiled and told us about the first child he had ever helped place. He had just made a visit to him at his school and said he was thriving. He told Jaime again she was doing a very courageous thing and that it was an admirable decision.

Then, after a short pause, he leaned over his desk and, with a smile and a twinkle in his eye, whispered, "That child is my grandson!"

❧ ☙

Jaime

The first week out of the hospital I felt more like an emotional time bomb than a human being. I would be cheerful and happy to be with my friends one moment and, in the next, I would be overcome by the love and deep sadness I felt not having my son with me. I missed Brennan more than words can express. *My son—my own flesh and blood.* I knew this was all a part of God's plan; that he was to be Dan and Kari's child to raise and love. But in no way did that mean I would have to stop loving him as my own.

One night before bed, Brooke, Christine, another friend Bethany, and I were hanging out together, lying on the bed talking while the "Downhere" CD we received as a Christmas gift played softly in the background. The song, "Calmer of the Storm," came on and as I listened to the words, I began sobbing, first quietly and then increasingly louder. I related to the words almost too well. They expressed exactly what I felt.

> *When everything is wrong*
> *The day has past and nothing's done*
> *When the whole world seems against me*
> *When I'm rolling in my bed*

There's a storm in my head
I'm afraid of sinking in despair

Teach me, Lord to have faith
In what You're bringing me will
Change my life and bring You glory

There on the storm
I am learning to let go
Of the will that I so long to control
There may I be in Your arms, eternally
I thank You, Lord
You are the Calmer of the storm
...
And oh when a torment blows
In the middle of the sea
May I never trust, never trust in me
'Cause in Your arms I find no tragedy

There on the storm
I am learning to let go
The white wave's high
It's crashing o'er the deck
And I don't know where to go
Where are You, Lord?
Is this ship going down?
The mast is gone so throw the anchor
Should I jump and try to swim to land?

There on the storm
Teach me God to understand
Of Your will that I just cannot control
There may I see all Your love protecting me
I thank You, Lord
You are the Calmer of the storm[25]

I soaked up every word. It was my heart's cry. *I am learning to let go of the will that I so long to control.*

Brooke came over with her blanket and lay next to me. Bethany and Christine came over and sat by the bed, each with one hand on me. None of them said a word. They didn't need to. They just prayed quietly and silently showed me their love and support. It was one of the most beautiful moments I had during my Mercy stay.

December 22 Prayer Journal Entry:

"Daddy, I was looking up 'comfort' today in your Word and found Jeremiah 31:13, 'I will turn their mourning into gladness, I will give them comfort and joy instead of sorrow.' Please do this in my life. I want to be happy and joyful! I don't know why, but I woke up today grieving for Brennan. I miss him, Daddy. I miss my baby boy. I know it's your will for him to be Dan and Kari's but this is really hard for me. I yearn to hold him in my arms; hold him close to me. Lord, please comfort me. Continue to give me peace about all this. My heart aches because I miss him so much.

"Jaime, my dear child. I am close to you. I am and will continue to comfort you through this. You are precious to Me and it hurts Me to see you cry for your little one. That's how I used to cry for you. I missed you so much and am overjoyed to have you back. I love you, Sweetie. You make me so proud! You're doing a wonderful job. Stay in My comfort, peace and joy."

Chapter 23

Family Christmas

❧ ☙

Lisa

This morning I checked out of the Candlewood and picked up Jaime from Mercy for her two-week Christmas vacation. Soon we were off to move into the Andersons' home, our Christmas "dream" home God had so wonderfully provided.

It was big…and beautiful…and handsomely decorated for Christmas. Just moving in was a lavish experience and we felt a bit like royalty. Overwhelmed and in awe once again of God's outpouring of love towards us, we were both elated. This home surpassed my dreams. It was everything on my list *and more*.

Brian joined us after work and we spent the weekend settling in. When the time came to pick Gene up from the airport on Monday, we were all excited. It seemed like forever since I'd seen him and I was glad he could finally be here with us. We ran to him as soon as he came out of the secured area and greeted him with possibly the longest family group hug in history.

We were all talking over each other, filling him in on all the things that had happened in the last couple of weeks. Later, we gave him the "tour" of the Andersons' home and let him unpack while we fixed dinner.

❧ ☙

Jaime

After dinner, we gathered in the gentleman's den and Dad said he had something for me. After explaining his surprise, he presented me with a beautiful necklace he had designed and had custom-made for me. It was breathtaking, and coming from my father, it meant a great deal to me. He told me he was so sorry he couldn't be with me during the past couple of weeks. It had been terribly hard on him, but he loved me dearly and was *proud of me*.

Those words still ring in my heart to this day. To hear my father say how proud he was of me meant *everything*. And the necklace? It will always remain one of my most cherished possessions.

~ ~

Lisa

I must admit this was a difficult Christmas for our family. We tried to keep things as normal as possible living in the balance between the strain of this whole experience on one side, and the awesomeness of all the Lord had done and the joy of being together again on the other.

We never really did talk much about our feelings. Perhaps they were still too fresh and too deep to express. I don't know, but from time to time I went back to that familiar place deep inside; that quiet place with the Lord formed way back in May at my mother's home when I first learned Jaime was pregnant. I loved withdrawing there, where I could simply sit in profound silence and soak in His presence.

Jaime frequently slipped into another world, somber and deep in thought. Besides all that had already transpired, she was distraught about Brennan having to spend his first Christmas between families. I'm sure she prayed for him constantly, as did I. We all trusted God to be with him, and looked forward to the adoption ceremony when he'd finally join his new family.

Thankfully, Gene was fresh to the whole scene and he and Brian kept things rolling for us. In addition to all the typical kinds of things a family must do to prepare for and celebrate the holidays, the house had a large game room and we spent hours there playing board games, ping pong, and pool. We reminisced about prior Christmases and favorite memories and from occasionally we'd remember additional bits of information about our last couple of weeks and shared it with Gene.

We also spent a couple of evenings with Dan and Kari. One evening they came over for dinner and games. We spent the other at Opryland Hotel going through the ice sculptures. Each time we got together with them we felt more and more like family, and I sensed they did too.

We were allowed two visits with Brennan before the adoption ceremony. The first one had been the prior week with just Jaime, Brian, and myself. Thankfully, Gene was able to join us for the second one. It felt strange visiting with Brennan in a conference room at Mercy, but we were grateful to have the time with him. We hovered around Jaime as she got him out of his carrier and watched her as she cuddled him in her arms and talked to him. She shared her time with him, letting us hold him for a while and we each loved having that little bundle in our arms. We treasured every minute, storing these memories with him deep in our hearts and trying not to think or talk about what was to come, The time flew quickly by and before we knew it, our visit with Brennan was over.

At some point during Jaime's ten days, I asked her how she was doing and if she had thought about changing her decision. We hadn't talked about her feelings much and I wanted to know where she stood with everything. She calmly and simply replied, "You know, Mother, if God hadn't done all these things for me—the signs, the dreams—I would be having a much harder time right now. But it is so *clear* to me this is His plan for Brennan. Dan and Kari are the parents God planned for him. Because of that, I can be strong."

Yes, she was right. God had made it very clear in so many different ways that this was His plan. He had been right in the middle of everything, and He was giving Jaime the strength to walk this out. Nevertheless, I knew that it was the hardest thing she'd ever had to do in her life, possibly the most difficult challenge she would ever have to face.

Jaime

Journal Entry, December 29:

Tomorrow is the big day – the adoption ceremony. I can't believe it's already here. It seems like just yesterday when I found out I was pregnant. Time has flown by these last seven months. Weird, but it seems I had Brennan months ago. Maybe it seems more like a dream. My mind is so flooded with emotions and thoughts. They all seem to run together. I feel handicapped in a way. Everything that has happened since May is flashing before my eyes.

Am I ready for this? I was planning on the adoption ceremony being in the middle of January. I have until tomorrow at 4 p.m. to change my decision. That's not God's will though. He has made it so clear to me—to everyone really. No more weekly visits. We are talking a LONG time before I see him again. As of tomorrow, he will be their son. No longer Brennan Maxwell, but Maxwell Brennan. He will not belong to me anymore; he won't be mine.

Lord, you have to help me through this! I don't ever want to fully lose him. I love him so much. This is my baby boy. I know this is the best for him and he'll be better off this way. I'm in no position at this point to parent a child. Plus, this is clearly Your will; Your will for his life, for my life, for Dan and Kari's lives. They're going to make awesome parents.

Daddy, give me peace and strength for tomorrow. Please give me grace and mercy. Be with me, comfort me, love me. I'm going to need it. Thank you!

Chapter 24

Adoption Ceremony

Monday, December 30

Finally, with everything completed, Brennan's adoption ceremony was scheduled for the first possible day after Jaime's ten days of waiting. Monday evening, December 30, Gene, Brian, Jaime and I arrived at the corporate offices of Mercy Ministries a little bit early to spend a final few minutes alone with Brennan. This visit had been arranged for us just prior to the ceremony, giving us a final opportunity to hold, hug and kiss him, tell him we love him, and say goodbye.

Jaime held him close as a staff member led us to a small room on the other side of the building. Dan and Kari, her parents, grandmother, and pastor had already arrived so we introduced ourselves and visited while waiting for Nancy Alcorn, Mercy's founder and president. They were delightful people, warm and caring, and I thanked the Lord that Brennan would grow up having them as his family.

Nancy welcomed us and opened our small and private ceremony with a prayer. She shared with us how God unfolded the vision for Mercy Ministries years before. Then she described how He had led and provided for every step, from its humble beginnings in a single home in Louisiana to several homes in the U.S. and international affiliates abroad.

I felt my admiration and gratitude growing for this bold woman of faith and her ministry. That remarkable woman—the head of this large ministry—was making time to meet with us and personally celebrate this very important event in our lives spoke volumes about her and her convictions. It also demonstrated to us how she felt about Jaime.

When she spent the next 20 minutes honoring Jaime, I was deeply grateful and a bit surprised. *Oh, Lord, I was certainly not expecting this.* She thanked her for her courage and determination. She told us about her commitment to do everything she was asked to do and how hard that was sometimes. She explained how unselfish her decision was to give the gift of life, of a family, to a couple who didn't have a way to become one. Finally, she told Jaime how very proud of her she was; that she was truly a hero.

Then, turning to Gene and me, she thanked us for being such strong and supportive parents and honored us with her comments. Next, she thanked Brian, who had been there with deep love and support for his sister and had reached out to the girls at Mercy with his kindness.

I treasured every bit of it. So often girls in this situation (and sometimes their families) are criticized and judged. But Jaime had continually experienced just the opposite: grace, forgiveness, understanding and unconditional love. *Oh, Lord, what a gift to have her honored and thanked.* It gave me a new appreciation for her.

And to be thanked and honored ourselves? It surprised and blessed me beyond belief to experience God's overflowing love like this.

After Nancy finished, she prayed...*for Jaime*...first. I realized I must have expected her to pray for Dan, Kari and Brennan first and it delighted me. We gathered around Jaime and laid hands on her as Nancy prayed.

Then she moved to Brennan, the quiet, precious little bundle in her arms, and prayed for him and then each of us, and finally for Dan and Kari.

I will never forget the moment Jaime kissed Brennan on his forehead, then turned to Kari and laid him gently in her arms for the final time. Dan moved next to her and they gazed down together on their new little son, love sparkling in their eyes. It was a tender moment, savored by all.

Dan and Kari thanked Jaime and surprised all of us by lavishing her with gifts. I must say, it endeared me even more to this dear couple. They had been so warm and caring, so solid in character; the perfect choice for our little grandchild.

They gave me a gift as well, a beautiful journal, and thanked me. Then it was our turn. We presented Dan and Kari with the Bible storybook we bought for Brennan and almost immediately Dan began pretending to read him his first Bible story, providing the perfect bit of comedy. *Yes, Kari will be a wonderful mother for Brennan, and Dan, a great father.*

By this time, so much peace enveloped our hearts that no tears came, just a quiet and tender settling, knowing this was the very *good plan*[26] of a loving and incredible God. The evening ended with deep, heartfelt joy, some laughter and an amazing sense of gratitude for all He had done.

☙ ❧

Jaime

It was such a precious time for all of us. Pleased beyond measure, I couldn't have asked for it to go any better than it did.

One of the most wonderful things Nancy said was, "What you see now coming out of Jaime was there the day she walked into Mercy. Mercy was the water that caused her to bloom, but the seed had already been planted and had begun sprouting before she arrived." She then turned to face my parents and thanked them for their support and love for me during this time, recognizing how important they were for my healing process.

Brian spoke up at one point and said how proud of me he was; that he had never been prouder of me. That meant so much to me, coming from my older brother.

After everyone had spoken their heart and we finished praying, I placed Brennan in Kari's arms. It was official. I noticed how peaceful he seemed in her arms, as if he knew she was his mother. It was wonderful to witness. It would have made it really hard if he had started crying, but he never did. He fell asleep after she gave him his bottle and it helped me beyond words to see how comfortable he was with them. I couldn't have chosen a better, more wonderful couple to raise my baby. God did an amazing thing when he matched us all together.

I wasn't expecting anything, so it certainly surprised me when they presented me with some gorgeous jewelry. How wonderfully thoughtful.

I gave them the baby blanket I had crocheted for Brennan over the previous couple of months and they loved it.

As the evening drew to an end, Kari and I sat talking quietly on the couch. I told her how much her genuine concern for me and my well-being meant to me.

We hugged one another and said goodbye. I had no idea when I would see them again, but it was finished. Brennan was now legally Dan and Kari's. He was now "Max," their son, and it felt good having him finally be with them, the couple God had handpicked to raise him. He was now home with his new family.

Chapter 25

Wrapping Up

❧ ❦

After the tumultuous ride of the previous months, life after the adoption ceremony seemed rather anticlimactic. We relaxed and enjoyed the last few days of our Christmas vacation together but, too soon, it all came to an end. Gene went back to work, Brian went back to his home, and Jaime and I wrapped up things at the Andersons' before she went back to Mercy. I flew home exactly one month to the day from when I left to come to Nashville. So much had happened since then.

It seemed as if it were years—another lifetime ago.

The day after the adoption ceremony was New Year's Eve. It struck me as significant that the Lord wrapped this all up in time for it to be behind us as we stepped into the new year. Brennan would begin his new life with his new name and new family. It would be a year of new beginnings for all of us.

Every bit of our "Mercy Month" had had been incredible. The whole pregnancy had been amazing, but these last few weeks, well, we hardly had adequate words for them. We are more in awe than ever of God and His great desire to love us and be involved in our lives.

We trusted Him with the situations at hand and saw the miraculous things He did. We loved and trusted Him before, but it grew to a much deeper level. We got to "*taste and see that He is good*"[27] and we will never be the same.

So how do you go back to normal life after that? You don't. You continue to look to God and trust Him. You make dreaming with Him more a part of your life. You expect Him to do the *"exceedingly, abundantly more than we can ever think or imagine[28]"* kinds of things in your lives and you *enjoy Him…*

…Forever.

*Now to Him,
who is able to do **super-abundantly**,
far over and above
all that we dare ask or think,
infinitely beyond our highest prayers, desires, thoughts, hopes,
or dreams —
to **Him** be glory!!!*
(Ephesians 3:20)[29]

☙ ❧

Chapter 26

Full Circle

☙ ❧

Jaime

I returned to Mercy excited to see my friends again and enthused about what the Lord had in store for me the next few months. I knew He still had a great deal of work to do in me and wanted me to remain pliable in His hands.

What the enemy meant for harm, the Lord turned around for such good. Getting pregnant at that time in my life turned out to be the best thing that could have happened to me. I sometimes wonder how different my life would have been if God had not allowed me to get pregnant. Now, a beautiful baby boy had entered this world and I was being transformed into a new person.

In those several months following the adoption ceremony, I received loving support as I worked through my grief and other issues God revealed in me—rejection, shame, anger and old places of hurt and wounding. Like refining gold with fire, He brought to the surface lies I had believed about myself and revealed other things operating in my life. I hadn't known *why* I was the way I was and how I found myself living a life so different from the one the Lord wanted. I didn't know what "issues" were or that people had them. I just thought that's the way people were. But through months of sessions with Cissy, my counselor, I received great healing and left equipped with tools to recognize the enemy's schemes, and to identify issues at the root and deal with them.

I graduated from Mercy Ministries on May 20—nine months after stepping through the doors—and although I had given my most precious gift to a wonderful and loving family, I did not leave empty-handed. I had experienced firsthand the beauty of the Lord and the intricate workings of His hands and learned of His faithfulness and goodness, His mighty power, overwhelming compassion, and intense love.

Although I would love to say I lived life without struggles after I left Mercy, I didn't. Regrettably, I made mistakes and occasionally wrestled with old ways and thought patterns. But with the tools I gained and the power of God's grace and forgiveness, I could work through them.

Having had my parents' love and support through this difficult time was crucial. They helped me carry the huge burden lying heavily on my shoulders and were a source of compassion and great stability. My relationship with my mother grew tremendously as we walked this journey and later wrote this book together—and I love her now more than ever.

My relationship with Dan, Kari, Max and his little brother, Logan, is a wonderful blessing. We now enjoy an open adoption, for which I am very grateful and I get to see them from time to time. I absolutely love watching Max grow up into a handsome and intelligent young man. Dan and Kari continue to amaze me with the way they parent and I could not be more pleased with God's choice of them.

One of my greatest fears had been that Max wouldn't remember me, but he seemed to sense the bond between us even at a young age. During a visit with him and Kari when he was three months old, he looked intently at me with those big blue eyes, making facial expressions and little noises like he was talking to me. We had an entire conversation without speaking a word, but I believe he knew exactly who I was. Early on, Dan and Kari told him I was his birthmother and he calls me "Miss Jaime." They have been the most amazing Godsend, respecting and honoring me from the day we met, and have walked this all out with great wisdom and thoughtfulness.

❧❦

Four years after graduating from Mercy, I married the man of my dreams. I had created a long list of things I desired in my husband, not unlike the one I did for Max's adoptive couple, and God proved as faithful to me with that list as He had the other.

I was concerned how my future husband would respond upon finding out I had a child I placed for adoption. But to my surprise and utter amazement, not only did Jeremy *not* respond in a negative or dismissive way, his response was heartfelt, loving, and tender and I could tell it moved him deeply. It was a beautiful moment. There was nothing to fear after all.

When we decided to start a family, we assumed it would happen rather immediately. Unfortunately, it didn't, and as the months dragged on and on, I became discouraged and began to lose hope as our dream of having a family drifted further and further away.

Then one day God reminded me of a time before Max was born when I was really struggling. *What if he ends up being the only child I'll ever have and I place him for adoption? I desire so much to be a mother. What if I'm not able to have more children or ever have another boy?* The Lord gently responded, "*Jaime, you will have a son of your own one day. Trust me.*"

After several miscarriages, I needed this hope to hold on to. However painful this road was, we trusted that when the timing was right, we would conceive. I had always hoped I would have a child before I turned 30, but a couple of months into my 29th year, I realized it probably wouldn't happen, so I let it go and put it in God's hands.

However, we soon discovered we were expecting again, but instead of holding our breath and fearing another miscarriage, we chose to trust the Lord. If this were His timing, we couldn't be more excited. But we sensed an overwhelming peace that if not, it would be okay and God would still keep His promise.

As each week went by we became more and more excited. *This is it.* We could not wait to become parents and to meet our baby. We were so excited when we found out we were expecting a boy. Walking out of the doctor's office, we ducked into an empty room and tears flooded our eyes as we hugged. Neither of us had said a word to each other, but we both had secretly hoped for a little boy. Faithful to His word, God was blessing me with one of my own.

Our son was born two weeks before my 30th birthday. Holding him for the first time brought an overwhelming feeling of love and a deep sense of awe. God's timing was spectacular. Not only did he bless me with a son before I turned 30, he gave me a special kiss from heaven as that year my birthday fell on Mother's Day.

Although I had him in the same hospital and with the same midwife group as Max, this experience was incredibly different than before. My husband was able to be there with me and we anticipated his birth together, as my mother had prayed. Also, not only did I give birth naturally without being on any medication, but not a single needle pierced my skin the entire time I was admitted. I did not have preeclampsia or the need to be induced. And by far, the most redeeming aspect of the whole experience was leaving the hospital holding my beautiful little son close to my heart instead of a little stuffed animal, knowing we had the rest of our lives to enjoy each other.

As Jeremy wheeled me out to the car, accompanied by my parents, Mother glanced at a clock in the lobby. "Honey, look at the clock! It's 5:07, the *exact* time you gave birth!" Grace and completion...

It was finished.

My heavenly Father, in His great love and faithfulness, brought my story full circle.

If you trust in the Lord and put your faith in Him; if you lay down your life and truly pray for His will instead of your own desires; He will guide you perfectly and will make beauty out of the ashes in your life.

> He *"bestows a crown of beauty instead of ashes*
> *The oil of joy instead of mourning,*
> *And the garment of praise instead of a spirit of heaviness.*
> *They will be called oaks of righteousness,*
> *A planting of the Lord*
> *For the display of His splendor."*[30]
> (Isaiah 61:3 NIV and NKJ)

Authors' Notes

☙ ❧

    We hope this story has touched you in a way that encourages and challenges you in whatever situation you may be facing and has shown you how amazing and wonderful God is. He wants to do the same kinds of things in your life as He did in ours. And He will, if you'll ask Him. He loves you whether you know Him yet or not, and He longs for you to know Him, *really* know Him.

    Invite Him into your life and your difficult circumstance and then trust Him to do impossible things. He is God *Almighty;* the one who can do the *impossible*. Ask Him to guide you, then listen and pay attention. He'll begin to speak to you and lead you in a way that is unique to only you.

    His love and power are enough to get you through anything you are facing. He'll never leave you and will never let you go. If you start heading down the wrong path, He'll gently nudge you back on track. Keep trusting Him and allow Him to come into your life and do the incredible. If you're already in the habit of trusting Him with things, stretch to trust Him with more. It will be an amazing adventure.

    In our case, it was an unplanned pregnancy, but it could be anything; a lost job, financial problems, a marriage in trouble, an eating disorder, abuse, drugs, prison or whatever else your situation may be. God is the same in every circumstance and His promises are the same for all of us. Our part is to believe them and trust Him; to go where and do what He leads us to.

    However, don't be in a rush. God's timing is perfect and often very different than ours. Look for the big picture and trust Him with it. This difficult situation in our lives was the *very thing* God used to turn me (Jaime) around, give Dan and Kari the desire of their hearts, and bring our family closer—healing us and strengthening our relationships. It took quite a while to pull off, but God did it. And, the bigger picture wasn't just the pregnancy, it was the answers God brought in so many areas of our lives, after years of praying and trusting Him.

We hope you'll let God have your bigger picture. Your part is simply to believe and trust. You will be astonished to see what He does.

Lisa and Jaime

Endnotes

Chapter 3
[1] For an explanation, see the beginning of Chapter 9 -Mercy Ministries

Chapter 4
[2] Raymond Badham, "Magnificent," Hillsong Live Worship, "Blessed," 2001 Hillsong Publishing, (Admin. in U.S. & Canada by Integrity's Hosanna! Music)

Chapter 5
[3] American Pregnancy Association, www.americanpregnancy.org, see ' Unplanned Pregnancy/Pregnancy Options
[4] Job 22:28 (NKJ)

Chapter 6
[5] Proverbs 3:5-6, (my version of the NIV)

Chapter 7
[6] Isaiah 55:9

Chapter 8
[7] Mercy Ministries / "Who We Are"/ Founder, Nancy Alcorn, www.mercyministries.com
[8] Mercy Ministries / "Who We Are"/ Founder, Nancy Alcorn, www.mercyministries.com
[9] www.mercyministries.com
[10] www.joycemeyer.org
[11] Psalms 46:1 NKJ

Chapter 12
[12] Psalms 37:4

Chapter 13
[13] Psalms 138:8
[14] Kathleen Silber, Dear Birthmother: Thank You for Our Baby, (Corona Publishing Co, 1999)

Chapter 14
[15] Philippians 4:7

Chapter 15
[16] Some of these names have been changed
[17] James 4:6 (AMP)

Chapter 19
[18] Ez. 16:6
[19] Her paraphrase of Ps. 118:17 NKJV
[20] 2 Corinthians 5:17
[21] Romans 8:35-39
[22] Romans 8:28

Chapter 20
[23] Isaiah 61:3

Chapter 21
[24] Jeremiah 29:11

Chapter 22
[25] Jason Ronald, Will Germain, Marc A. Martel, "Calmer of the Storm," Downhere, "Downhere", © 2001 Word Music, LLC., Slyngshot Records

Chapter 24
[26] Jeremiah 29:11

Chapter 25
[27] Psalms 34:8
[28] Paraphrased from Ephesians 3:20
[29] Ephesians 3:20

Chapter 26
[30] Isaiah 61:3 NIV and NKJ

Authors Contact

※

For more information regarding the book or speaking engagements, visit:

www.MotherAreYouSittingDown.com

www.ingramcontent.com/pod-product-compliance
Lightning Source LLC
Chambersburg PA
CBHW050552300426
44112CB00013B/1885